CHURCHILL
— ON —
LEADERSHIP

EXECUTIVE SUCCESS IN
THE FACE OF ADVERSITY

STEVEN F. HAYWARD

GRAMERCY BOOKS
NEW YORK

This 2004 edition is published by Gramercy Books, an imprint of Random House Value Publishing, a division of Random House, Inc., New York, by arrangement with Crown Publishers, a division of Random House, Inc.

Gramercy is a registered trademark and the colophon is a trademark of Random House, Inc.

Random House
New York • Toronto • London • Sydney • Auckland
www.randomhouse.com

Printed and bound in the United States

A catalog record for this title is available from the Library of Congress.

ISBN 0-517-22326-0

10 9 8 7 6 5 4 3 2 1

To Dad, who knew everything . . .

CONTENTS

PREFACE

THIS BOOK OWES its inspiration to cognitive dissonance—the mental disorientation that arises from contrasting modes of thought. In my particular case, the story begins during my years in graduate school, where, to make ends meet, I held a job as editor of a regional monthly business magazine, covering businesses and businesspeople in the booming "Inland Empire" region of southern California.

The cognitive dissonance arose from having to change mental gears so abruptly and completely each day. Mornings, I would be absorbed, either with books or in the classroom, by the serious study of history and politics. At Claremont Graduate School in the 1980s, this study often turned to Churchill and other great statesmen. It is through the study of great statesmen such as Churchill and Lincoln and the American founders that the study of political life and political ideas best comes to life, and Claremont in those years offered the opportunity to spend time with scholars who made the lives and teachings of great statesmen especially vivid.

In the afternoons, the course of producing a monthly business magazine brought me into regular contact—through interviews, lunches, and business civic affairs—with businesspeople who were largely uninterested in politics and ignorant of history. I say this not to revive the affected snobbery that businesspeople are philistines. On the contrary, I regard entrepreneurs as engaged in heroic undertakings, albeit often on a small scale. But it is natural that people preoccupied with the practical necessities and the stress of building a business would not necessarily spend their scarce leisure hours reading the same kind of books and thinking about the same kind of questions that I did. Churchill himself had written that "a man's Life must be nailed to a cross either of Thought or Action" (though this was a noble lie as applied to himself, since he was a man of both), and as man of thought I held no snobbish disdain for the people of practical commercial action I met each day.

Yet even the most preoccupied citizen will think of politics occasionally, and so from time to time, especially as my other life became known among the businesspeople I wrote about, conversation would turn to politics. And while opinions and perceptions of political issues were predictably all over the map, the lament that contemporary political life lacked leaders was commonplace. Almost equally commonplace, at least among the generation ahead of mine, was the sentiment that boiled down to something like: "Now Churchill: *There* was a man!"

My poor interview subjects and lunch partners had no idea what they had let themselves in for. This was better than dessert—"like breaking the bank at Monte Carlo," as Churchill himself once remarked about a minor personal triumph. Most people had little knowledge of Churchill beyond the fact that he had "stood up to Hitler" and had given stirring speeches—"fight on the beaches" and so forth. As I offered details about how Churchill approached certain kinds of problems, about his perceptions of organizational behavior, about how he managed the various government departments he led in his long career, I began to see that Churchill's story offers valuable lessons for executives and entrepreneurs. Many was the time that a businessperson would call back asking again for the details of a Churchill story I had told.

Having finally finished my Ph.D., I moved on from business journalism to the world of nonprofit public policy think tanks, a career more in harmony with my academic background. But even nonprofit organizations (*especially* nonprofit organizations, my graduate school landlord Peter Drucker argues) require sound management and leadership skills. And so I recently spent a day in an executive management seminar with Brian Tracy, one of the preeminent figures in the field. (His hot-selling books and tapes include titles such as *How to Master Your Time*, *The Psychology of Achievement*, and *The Laws of Success*.) Brian used Churchill stories and quotations throughout his presentation, though in nearly every case it seemed I had another story or apposite quotation, usually from an earlier phase of Churchill's career. Brian, like most people, looks mostly at the pinnacle of Churchill's life—his time as prime minister during World War II. But I have always found Churchill's early career, especially his disappointment and humiliation in World War I, not only more interesting in some ways but also essential to understanding how he approached the problems of leading the government and the war effort in World War II. I'm sure Brian was thoroughly annoyed with my repeated interruptions, but during conversation at the end of the day he suggested that I ought to write a book about the subject of Churchill's management and leadership style.

At first blush it seemed to me that the last thing the world needs is another book on Churchill. My own collection of books by or about Churchill dominates my not inconsiderable library. But in a world that can support a book on *Lincoln and the Coming of the Caterpillar Tractor* as well as *Lincoln on Leadership*, perhaps there is indeed room for a book on Sir Winston's leadership style. (*The Seven Highly Effective Habits of Churchill* perhaps?) In the vast and growing literature about leadership, Churchill is almost invisible. One recent book on leadership from Harvard University Press discusses Hitler's leadership qualities for several pages but makes no mention of Churchill in the entire text. Other more contemporary figures—Nelson Mandela for example—are evidently more popular in the genre. The only sensible thing I could find about Churchill's lessons for business executives was a short article by Srully Blotnick in *Forbes* magazine ("Churchill on Management," October 21, 1985).

The Introduction explores the appropriateness of Churchill as a fit subject for the burgeoning field of leadership studies. Suffice it to say here that this effort is intended to be more than an excuse for a potted biography of the great man. It is unavoidable that this enterprise involves retelling much of the Churchill story, though I have sought to do so in a new way. I have followed a rule in the writing of this book to avoid simply retailing stories that appear in other Churchill books. I have sought to omit from this account many of the well-known anecdotes and familiar quotations by or about Churchill that appear with high frequency in the existing books about him, except in cases where one is essential to making a key point. Instead, I have combed the documentary record, chiefly the memoranda, letters, and speeches that have been published as companion volumes to Martin Gilbert's official biography, for overlooked material that bears on the central question here—Churchill's executive style. Gilbert has assembled 14 of these companion volumes (with more on the way); the collection comprises more than 15,000 pages, and is a treasure trove of material illuminating in detail how Churchill actually conducted many important matters. Churchill once remarked that "writing a book is an adventure. To begin with it is a toy and an amusement. Then it becomes a mistress, then it becomes a master, then it becomes a tyrant. The last phase is that just as you are about to be reconciled to your servitude, you kill the monster and fling him to the public." This book was a mistress throughout, and never became a tyrant or even a master, on account of the wonder inspired by the subject, combined with the professional excuse to go through so much of the Churchill literature and documents with greater care than usual.

As this is a thematic examination, many interesting details of the Churchill story have been left out. This book passes over several of the great political controversies involving Churchill, except where those controversies bear on some aspect of his leadership qualities or his organizational abilities. The Appendix covers the outlines of Churchill's career in enough detail to place the rest of this book in context, but I hope that readers who are unfamiliar with Churchill will also seek out one of the major biographies. The official biography, begun by Randolph Churchill and completed by Martin Gilbert, is—at eight volumes and more than 9,000 pages—probably too long for most readers, but Gilbert has produced a one-volume biography that is indispensable. William Manchester's two-volume biography, *The Last Lion* (a third volume of which is pending), is also a good introduction to the great man. Interested readers should not neglect Churchill's own writings—he did, after all, earn his principal income throughout his life as a writer. Especially recommended is *My Early Life*, a splendid autobiography of his life up until his marriage in 1908 (following which, as he ended the book, he "lived happily ever afterwards"), and *Thoughts and Adventures*, a collection of essays originally published in the 1930s, a wonderful introduction to his perspicacity of thought. Both books are still in print. One-volume condensations are recently available of his two long multivolume works, *The World Crisis*, about World War I, and *The Second World War*, for which he was awarded the Nobel Prize for Literature.

Calvin Coolidge—a much underrated man—once remarked that "Great men are the ambassadors of Providence sent to reveal to their fellow men their unknown selves. . . . When the reverence of this nation for its great men dies, the glory of the nation will die with it." As the firsthand knowledge of the great wars of the 20th century fades and our attention turns increasingly to more contemporary people and issues, it is fitting to revive again what Churchill once called, in speaking of his own father, "a certain splendid memory."

INTRODUCTION

The World of Politics and the World of Commerce—What Business Leaders Can Learn from the Great Statesmen

———◆◆◆———

Q: "What makes a good manager?"

A: "I prefer the term business leader."

—JACK WELCH, CEO, GENERAL ELECTRIC CORPORATION

T HERE IS NO more dramatic example of leadership and executive action than the premiership of Winston Churchill during World War II. The contrast between his prewar warnings about "the gathering storm" and the pusillanimous direction provided by his predecessors has etched a lasting lesson for international statecraft. The very term *appeasement*—an idea the young Churchill supported in some circumstances—now carries a strong stigma, while Churchill's prescient warnings—much criticized and resented at the time—are now regarded as the model of foresight and courage.

While Churchill's story is an example of leadership ability at its highest level, to apply his story for general purposes is to assume a heavy burden. It would be too trite to liken Churchill's circumstances in May 1940 to a corporate turnaround situation. The pinnacle of Churchill's career involved the weighty issues of war, statecraft, and national survival, and it may not be immediately apparent how Churchill's example translates to more ordinary circumstances, especially circumstances of everyday business and commerce. Churchill was, after all, a politician, and the world of politics seems remote from the world of business (the more remote, the better, most businesspeople would say). In the world of politics, the balance sheet is opaque (at best), while the profit and loss statement is nonexistent. On the contrary, the political world is disorderly, inefficient, undisciplined, and at times even irresponsible. Moreover, given that most politicians are masters of equivocation, it is hard to see what lessons business leaders can learn from politicians, most of whom seem to be models neither of leadership nor of basic managerial skill.

What probably rankles most business executives about the world of politics is the diffusion of responsibility and accountability. This seeming lack of accountability is a function of partisanship as well as of our democratic constitutionalism, in which the separation of powers among the three branches of government provides an institutional basis for finger-pointing and blame-shifting. In business, by contrast, there is no separation of powers—the entrepreneur or the CEO bears full responsibility and accountability. There can be no finger-pointing or blame-shifting. Think of how the term *office politics* is a low term, a term of contempt, derision, and disgust. If anything, the most popular idea afoot today is that we should shove aside the professional politicians and put business executives in charge of the government to "sort out the mess in Washington." What can a business executive expect to learn from studying politicians?

A lot. Paradoxically, it is precisely because a politician lacks the clear bottom-line standard of profit that public office requires superior leadership skills. While the business executive can look to the bottom line as to a North Star, the political executive confronts a Milky Way of competing and shifting priorities, requiring a full measure of judgment, vision, and persuasive skills. It is because so few people in politics have these skills in sufficient measure that we rarely laud politicians with the exalted term *statesman*.

Political skills can be extremely useful to a business executive, and not just for coping with the grubby business of "office politics." A senior business executive, no less than a political executive, finds it necessary to inspire and persuade, to reorganize, to probe after details and to delegate responsibility, to deal with the egos and

character flaws of individuals, all the while having in mind how all
the pieces of the organization and the plans fit into a larger whole. It
is a common mistake to think that structure, process, and reorganization will suffice to solve a business problem, when what is really
wanting is leadership, firmness, confidence, and direction. Almost
any scheme of organization can be made to work if there is effective leadership at the top. The example of Churchill provides rich
material for reflecting on these attributes.

The example of Churchill is additionally instructive because he
reached his pinnacle as a *war* leader. The parallels between warfare
and the world of commerce are quite deep, and today the idea of
business leadership goes hand-in-hand with the idea of strategy. The
Cuban Missile Crisis of 1962 has become a leading case study in
"crisis management," for example. The awareness of this parallel
has been growing on business authors for some years now. Peter
Drucker tells that when he wrote a book about business strategy in
the early 1960s, "I found that the word [strategy] could not be used
in the title without serious risk of misunderstanding. Booksellers,
magazine editors, and senior business executives all assured us that
'strategy' for them meant the conduct of military or election cam-
paigns," and was therefore foreign to their concerns.

Just as competitive behavior remains an essential aspect of
human nature, so too does the world of commerce mimic certain
aspects of organized warfare. Commonplace phrases such as "price
war" and "killing the competition" are more than just metaphors.
And even though commerce is nonviolent, it is not without casualties
from time to time in the form of layoffs, lost jobs, and destroyed
investment capital.

It is for reasons such as these that Churchill once remarked,
"There were very few things in military administration which a business man of common sense and little imagination could not understand if he turned his attention to the subject." At the most simple

level, consider that the two most basic initiatives in warfare are the concentrated offensive against an enemy's weak point and the maneuver around an exposed flank. It does not require a fanciful imagination to see the equivalents of these two basic strategies in the world of competitive commerce. The forward offensive resembles direct, head-to-head price competition, while the flanking maneuver is analogous to overtaking your competition by opening or exploiting a new market. In commercial competition as in a real battlefield offensive, you win by fighting more efficiently and cheaply than your foe, that is, by imposing unacceptable costs on your competitor. You also win through innovation—through technological improvements over your competitor's product. The rapid development of the personal computer and the fierce competition among PC companies over the last two decades in many ways resembles the evolution of offensive weaponry, which changed battlefield conditions dramatically and repeatedly over the last 1000 years. The debate during World War I about whether zeppelins (blimps) or the fast-developing airplanes would be the superior weapon for aerial warfare looks a lot like the debate over mainframe versus PC desktop computers a few years ago. And Hewlett-Packard provides a good example of a successful flanking maneuver in this same industry with its tactic of specializing in printers in addition to PCs. Apple Computer's Macintosh proprietary standard might be regarded as either a straight-ahead offensive or a flanking maneuver, and the failure to employ fully one strategy or the other is perhaps one reason why Apple has run aground lately. Meanwhile, as the PC makers slug it out, the high technology world waits keenly to see if a company can employ the Internet in a flanking strategy around Microsoft's dominance.

So the world of commerce like the world of warfare requires a CEO—a commander—who has the ability to comprehend the whole scene in strategic terms. Such a person must also inspire confidence and energy among the workforce, whether a marching army or the employees of a company. The characteristics and methods of what we call here "strategic insight" are susceptible to study and example.

Finally, it is useful to place the revived interest in leadership skills in a broader context. The recent interest in the idea of leadership is a healthy and welcome development. It is ironic that the interest in leadership studies should be burgeoning at the very same time that the role of the "great man" has fallen totally out of fashion with professional historians and social scientists. This is a sign that the academic scribblers, who fancy themselves to be in the avant garde of everything, are far behind the times. Practical people of commerce are embracing the value of the strength of character found in great leaders while the scribblers of the ivory tower are employing a decayed version of the reductionist way of thinking about the world that was fashionable in business 75 years ago. While the scribblers chatter on that the world is determined by impersonal forces, business leaders today have come to see ever more clearly the essential role of personal forces in shaping our destiny.

Beginning with the emergence of large-scale business enterprise a century ago, the art of administration, whether in private enterprise or in the public sector, emphasized *managerialism*, which, stripped to is barest essentials, consists mostly in the reduction of all tasks to bureaucratic routine. Managers, especially middle managers, were basically interchangeable so long as the routine and the process were in place. The impersonal forces of matter, rather than the personal forces of individuals, were thought to determine the shape and direction of progress in the modern world. The apotheosis of this "managerial revolution" was Frederick Taylor's famous time-and-motion study technique, which attempted to achieve maximum productive efficiency by essentially turning workers into robots. Taylorism found its equivalent in executive management with the coming of systems analysis and other quantitative abstractions, in which senior managers—often completely detached from the actual process of production or sales—would steer a large enterprise solely according to complex quantitative models.

Quantitative management certainly has its place, and can be highly effective for certain kinds of administrative tasks. Churchill was an early enthusiast of statistics and quantitative measures, as we shall see. But quantitative analysis is no substitute for leadership. For example, Robert McNamara relied heavily on systems analysis as president of Ford Motor Company in the late 1950s, and is said to have prided himself on *not* knowing how a car was actually built on the assembly line, which he seldom if ever visited. The defects of systems analysis became more evident when McNamara went from Ford to the Pentagon just in time for the Vietnam War, where it became readily apparent that he did not know how wars are actually fought in the field either.

McNamara's is the epitome of a managerial style now deservedly passing from the scene. Hence, his name does not appear much in the growing literature on executive leadership, despite his long and distinguished career in several glittering posts. Today it is obvious for anyone with eyes to see that bigger is not always better. Whereas popular thinking just 25 years ago still held that consolidation into huge conglomerates was the commercial future of the world—that bigger was at least inevitable, if not better—today in the era of downsizing, dynamic international competition, and overnight entrepreneurial start-ups, we increasingly prize the swashbuckling, risk-taking character of the entrepreneur over the bureaucracy of the manager. Even large enterprises today need to be able to transform themselves quickly with the same nimbleness as small companies. This requires above all the force of personal leadership rather than the ability to count beans.

The force of personal leadership is ironically even beginning to be quantified by the bean-counters. Holman W. Jenkins Jr. noted in a recent *Wall Street Journal* article that "An elegant study by Thor Thorlindsson, at the University of Iceland, found that about

40 percent of the variation in the herring catch among boats in the country's 200-strong fishing fleet depended on the person of the captain." Another recent study of large corporations over a four-year period by three scholars at the Wharton School of Finance concluded that between 15 percent and 25 percent of the variation in profitability was determined by the character of their chief executives. As Professor Robert J. House of Wharton concludes: "We're learning again what the military has known for thousands of years: Leadership is important."

A close look at Churchill's leadership style provides fresh vindication for the basic axiom of synergy—that the whole is greater than the sum of the parts. Indeed, Churchill himself often suggested that the genius of a great leader consists in the "constant harmony" of holding a variety of great purposes in mind all at once. In the account that follows, we shall dissect the harmonious mix of personal attributes, principles, and practices that contributed to Churchill's success as a leader, and recombine them at the end to appreciate the whole of what has often been called the *Churchillian style.*

CHAPTER I

THE KEYS TO UNDERSTANDING CHURCHILL

———◆◆◆———

*An accepted leader has only to be sure of what it is best to do,
or at least to have made up his mind about it.*
—WINSTON S. CHURCHILL, 1949

LEADERSHIP IS DIFFICULT enough to define concisely. Can leadership be learned in the same way as accounting or marketing? Churchill himself had doubts about this, once writing about military command that "genius . . . cannot be acquired, either by reading or experience." Seminars and even field programs designed to impart leadership skills are a burgeoning industry. Such programs often feature exercises such as persuading a group of people to drink a glass of green buttermilk (designed to teach how to overcome resistance), or exercises simulating aspects of the wilderness survival training that military commandos go through.

Such exercises may be useful, but the question of leadership is at once both more complicated and more simple. Although the deep insight that completes the genius of a great leader is perhaps not something that one can acquire through study or even experience, much of the task of leadership depends on the old-fashioned virtue or character of the individual who would lead.

Every now and then a magazine or journal will survey CEOs and other senior professionals about the top ingredients for leadership. Not surprisingly, *character* regularly shows up near the top of almost everyone's list. Other ingredients that show up with high regularity on such lists are judgment, ability to inspire, empathy, toughness, and intelligence. These and other traits that may be mentioned are all really subordinate aspects of character.

In the case of Churchill, four essential aspects of character were the key to his leadership. The four aspects that set him apart from ordinary politicians were candor and plain speaking, decisiveness, the ability to balance attention to details with a view of the wider scene, and a historical imagination that informed his judgment.

Candor and Plain Speaking

The ordinary politician is a master of equivocation in public pronouncements, for the obvious reason that a politician whose chief goal is to be reelected over and over again will wish to avoid antagonizing any group of voters. Churchill often commented upon this aspect of conventional political life. He remarked early in his career that the most desirable qualification for a politician "is the ability to foretell what is going to happen tomorrow, next week, next month, and next year—and to have the ability afterwards to explain why it didn't happen." Politicians have to confine themselves to platitudes, Churchill remarked, because the politician usually represents a compromise. It is not safe to go far beyond "The sun shone yesterday upon this great and glorious country. It shines today and will shine tomorrow." This fundamental aspect of political life is confirmed by the fact that politicians who are candid and plain-spoken—politicians who are not a bland compromise—are usually disliked by the public even more strongly than average politicians. Newt Gingrich serves as a current example of this phenomenon; his unpopularity derives in large part from his extraordinary bluntness and candor about what he thinks.

Churchill was far from being a bland compromise, and this explains a large measure of the distrust and animosity he generated among his colleagues and among the public throughout his long career. "What is the good of speaking one language if you can't put your differences to each other plainly?" he once asked. "I decline utterly," he said of his aversion to equivocation and issue straddling, "to be impartial as between the fire brigade and the fire." Churchill's ability was always recognized, even by his harshest critics. But he took strong positions on the issues without the slightest regard for the often dominant contrary current of public opinion. Sophisticated people in the 1930s ridiculed Churchill for the seemingly simpleminded way he referred to Hitler as "that Bad Man." During the war he remarked, "A Hun alive is a war in prospect." In a speech shortly before his most humiliating election loss, he defiantly proclaimed: "This is no time for windy platitudes and glittering advertisements. The Conservative Party had far better go down telling the truth and acting in accordance with the verities of our position than gain a span of shabbily-bought office by easy and fickle froth and chatter." Churchill lived up to this standard right after the war in one of his most infamous election speeches, where he said that the Labour Party could not implement socialist measures in Britain without "some form of Gestapo," under which Britain's civil servants would be "no longer servants and no longer civil." Churchill's remark was inspired by Fredrich Hayek's recently published and now famous book, *The Road to Serfdom*, and though he was advised that people would bitterly resent the Gestapo reference, he insisted on using it anyway.

His candor extended to the invective he used against many of his contemporaries and colleagues, such as his comparison of socialist Prime Minister Ramsay MacDonald to the circus attraction, "the boneless wonder." Concerning Arthur Balfour, Churchill remarked: "If you wanted nothing done, Arthur Balfour was the best man for the task. There was no one equal to him." Regarding Prime Minister Stanley Baldwin, whose support of disarmament in the 1930s Churchill bitterly criticized, Churchill remarked: "Occasionally he stumbled over the truth, but hastily picked himself up and hurried on as if nothing had happened." He once lumped MacDonald and Baldwin together with the remark that they were "two nurses fit to keep silence around a darkened room." When someone compared

Neville Chamberlain and Clement Attlee to a snake dominating a rabbit, Churchill modified the comparison, saying, "It's more like a rabbit dominating a lettuce!" (Churchill also said that Attlee was a modest man; with much to be modest about, and on another occasion when Attlee was going abroad, that Attlee was no doubt afraid that when the mouse was away the cats would play.) About American Secretary of State John Foster Dulles: "He is the only case I know of a bull who carries his china closet with him." He also referred to him as "Dull, Duller, Dulles."

His candor and blunt-spokenness sparked much of the criticism against him throughout his career. "Winston thinks with his mouth," Prime Minister Herbert Asquith said of him in 1910. "He is impulsive and borne along on the flood of his all too copious tongue." Another colleague, offended by his bluntness, said that "Churchill really degrades public life more than anyone of any position in politics." Because of this candor, even his friends doubted his judgment. "He is the sort of man," one friend wrote of him early in his career, "whom, if I wanted a mountain to be moved, I should send for at once. I think, however, that I should not consult him after he had moved the mountain if I wanted to know where to put it."

But it was Churchill's forthrightness that was to serve him and his country so well when the hour of crisis came. Churchill's candor was a manifestation of his confidence in himself. He seldom had regrets about any position he had taken, even if events subsequently proved him wrong, or put him on the losing side of an issue. He once remarked, "In the course of my life I have often had to eat my words, and I must confess that I have always found it a wholesome diet."

Decisiveness

In addition to equivocation, the other dominant aspect of conventional political life is *temporization*. Politicians hate to make decisions, and almost always put off making a decision until compelled to do so. When possible, a politician will attempt to make a compromise decision, a decision based on the lowest common denominator such that the decision will offend the fewest people or interests. Moreover, politicians like to diffuse the responsibility for decisions, so that they will be able to spread the blame if something goes wrong. (This is part of the reason for bipartisanship.) Churchill, on the other hand, was *decisive*. He *liked* to make decisions, and to take full responsibility for them. He admired other leaders who were decisive. He was impressed on his first meeting with President Harry Truman in 1945 by Truman's "obvious power of decision."

Churchill seldom made decisions through the same kind of process that most other politicians use. He abhorred procrastination, temporization, equivocation, and crass interest-group calculation. "Unlike many politicians," Paul Addison observed of Churchill, "he never shrank from conflict when he believed that an issue had to be resolved." One of Churchill's favorite maxims was "ponder, and then *act*." He hated tentativeness and second-guessing. "Whatever course was decided upon," he urged repeatedly in the early days of World War II, "it was essential that we should now act decisively." Certainly he never displayed doubts after making a decision. He was a sound sleeper (and napper). He liked to say: "It is in my character that the nearer I get to the event, the more resolute I become." Another of his favorite axioms was "half-measures are vain."

Controversy swirls around many of Churchill's decisions. With such a long and varied career, he was closely involved in a great many decisions, either as the responsible executive with full discretion to make decisions, or more often as a part of the cabinet or cabinet committee, in which circumstances his confidence and resolve to reach clear decisions often irritated his more conventional, temporizing colleagues. His long public record, clarity, and forcefulness leave him easily exposed to second-guessing and criticism.

Few critics ever put his decisions into perspective, or in comparison with other politicians who eschewed clear decision. His friend Lord Birkenhead once remarked that "Winston was often right, but when he was wrong, well, my God." No one ever said such a thing about his contemporaries.

Surveys of business decision making have found that a startlingly high proportion of decisions—as much as 70 percent according to one survey by the American Management Association—turn out to be bad ones. Most business decisions happen away from public view; while sometimes fraught with large financial consequences, they do not often affect large numbers of the public in a direct and visible way. Rare is the business decision that is as large in its public consequences as a national political decision, but on those occasions—the decision to produce the "New Coke" is a superb example—the comparison of decision factors between business and politics is instructive. A public man whose decisions are always under close scrutiny could not survive even a 50 percent rate of incorrect or bad decisions (though Churchill reportedly once remarked, with apt words for entrepreneurs, that "success is going from failure to failure without loss of enthusiasm"). This is one reason politicians seek to diffuse responsibility for decisions. Churchill's decisions were more often right than wrong, I argue, but more important than the soundness of each individual decision is the process by which he chose courses of action (which will be discussed more fully in Chapter 6).

A leading reason for Churchill's decisiveness was that he was keenly aware how difficult it is to make things happen given the resistance and inertia of human organizations. "Most great exploits," he wrote shortly after World War I, "have to be [conducted] under conditions of peculiar difficulty and discouragement." "How easy to do nothing," he wrote in 1915, "How hard to achieve anything." Good ideas are not sufficient; drive, decision and follow-through are equally important, yet often insufficiently appreciated. "There are plenty of good ideas if only they can be backed with power and brought into reality," Churchill wrote to Arthur Conan Doyle (creator of Sherlock Holmes) during World War I. It was this drive to overcome the inertia typical of any collective organization that misled many observers into thinking that Churchill's principle was action for action's sake alone. This is an exaggeration, however. True enough, Churchill said during World War II that "I never worry about action, but only about inaction," but he counseled delay and even inaction on many occasions when his judgment told him that action of any kind would be unwise. Churchill understood that there are "immense walls of prevention" to almost any idea or plan that may take shape during difficult times. At a frustrating moment during World War II, Churchill said, "The difficulty is not winning the war; it is persuading people to let you win it—persuading fools."

Churchill's resolute and unflinching nature was exactly the reason he was a great leader, and why the example of politicians like Churchill or Abraham Lincoln or George Washington can from time to time redeem the realm of politics from mediocrity, cynicism, and suspicion of ambition and power. Reflecting after World War II, Churchill wrote, "Power, for the sake of lording it over fellow-creatures or adding to personal pomp, is rightly judged base." He had already supplied the answer to this common perception of the base motives of politicians in another passage written nearly 20 years before: "The pursuit of power with the capacity and in the desire to exercise it worthily is among the noblest of human occupations."

A crucial lesson of Churchill's story (which applies equally to most other statesmen who can be mentioned) is that his leadership gifts required a sufficiently large scope to be fruitful. Churchill was not well-suited for any position but chief executive, and his energy, drive, and encyclopedic mind, when exercised in the many subordinate positions he held throughout his career, alienated many of his colleagues and superiors. In a sense, Churchill's rocky career resulted in part from his not being promoted fast enough to the top (though with different luck he might have become prime minister during World War I or in the 1920s). Some of his colleagues recognized this early on. Sir Edward Grey, foreign secretary during World War I, once remarked that "Winston, very soon, will become incapable from sheer activity of mind of being anything in a Cabinet but Prime Minister." His restlessness and frustration, borne of his unsuitability for subordinate roles, misled nearly everyone about his leadership capabilities when the time came for him to assume the premiership in May 1940. His ascendancy to the premiership was viewed with dread and alarm by many of his peers, who, as Sir Ian Jacob was to reflect years later, "had not the experience or imagination to realize the difference between a human dynamo when humming on the periphery and when driving at the center." When "driving at the center," Churchill's decisiveness emerged as the vital quality required for national leadership.

Historical Imagination

The third important key to Churchill was his historical imagination. "The longer you look back," he wrote, "the farther you can look forward." The British historian Sir John H. Plumb wrote, "History, for Churchill, was not a subject like geography or mathematics, it was a part of his temperament, as much a part of his being as his social class and, indeed, closely allied to it . . . it permeated everything which he touched, and it was the mainspring of his politics and the secret of his immense mastery." In a famous essay titled "Winston Churchill in 1940," Isaiah Berlin wrote, "Churchill's dominant category, the single, central, organizing principle of his moral and intellectual universe, is a historical imagination so strong, so comprehensive, as to encase the whole of the present and the whole of the future in a framework of a rich and multicolored past." At a moment of particular frustration in the 1920s, Churchill wrote to a friend: "How strange it is that the past is so little understood and so quickly forgotten. We live in the most thoughtless of ages. Every day headlines and short views. I have tried to drag history up a little nearer to our own times in case it should be helpful as a guide in present difficulties." Therefore it was entirely in character when, during World War II, Churchill said that Hitler should study English history and contemplate his doom.

Churchill himself did not come by his historical imagination spontaneously. He wrote several volumes of history, including the four-volume *History of the English-Speaking Peoples*. He wanted to write a biography of Napoleon, and probably would have done so had not World War II intervened. Among the many researches Churchill conducted was his detailed and exhaustive study of his own ancestor, John Churchill, Duke of Marlborough, who led the armies of the Grand Alliance against the French in the early 18th century. Churchill's four-volume biography of his great ancestor, *Marlborough—His Life and Times*, is a classic of historical writing in its own right. Though Churchill wrote many fine books on military and political themes, *Marlborough* combines both war and politics at their highest level of understanding. The political philosopher Leo Strauss once described Churchill's *Marlborough* as "the greatest historical work written in our century, an inexhaustible mine of political wisdom and understanding, which should be required reading for every student of political science." It is a shame that it is not more widely read today, because it is the key to understanding Churchill, especially at his zenith during World War II.

In fact, *Marlborough*—which Churchill wrote during his "Wilderness Years" out of office in the 1930s—reads like an uncanny foreshadowing of Churchill's war leadership, to come just a few years later. For example, Churchill's contemporaries and subsequent historians have strained to explain his complex character. In *Marlborough* Churchill sought to unravel "the unfathomable mystery which Marlborough's character presents." Churchill's calm and steady demeanor throughout the trials of war has always been noted, as has his effect on the morale of those who worked around him. Marlborough, Churchill tells us, "preserved an imperturbable demeanor. . . . His appearance, his serenity, his piercing eye, his gestures, the tones of his voice—nay, the beat of his heart—diffused a harmony upon all around him. Every word he spoke was decisive." Marlborough also sounded notes of steely resolve that Churchill would echo in his own legendary speeches of defiance in 1940. Early in his command Marlborough commented, "The issue in this matter is victory or death." ("What a strange thing heredity is," Churchill once wrote to his wife in a different context. "We are really only variants of what has gone before.")

The circumstances in which Marlborough maneuvered in the 18th century also bear an uncanny resemblance to the circumstances Churchill faced during World War II. Marlborough, like Churchill, had to lead within the framework of an alliance with the armies of several other nations against a common foe. The war involved virtually the whole of civilized Europe at that time. Churchill's description of the strategic situation Marlborough faced is identical to the situations Churchill faced in both World War I and World War II: "In a war involving nearly the whole world it was natural that each campaign should offer to both sides a wide choice of plans, for and against any one of which there was much to be said. Each plan had to be weighed not only on its own merits, but in relation to all the others in the general setting of the war." Marlborough, like Churchill in the 20th century, "never ceased to think of the war as a whole."

As we shall see in the chapters ahead, this problem dominated Churchill in both world wars, and Churchill had a set of principles and guidelines from which to evaluate strategic options. Deciding what kind of forces to commit and where, along with the need to persuade your allies and partners of the wisdom of the initiative, is akin to making business decisions about how much of what kind of product to produce, and where it should be marketed, and how it can be done with partners in a joint venture. Just as the supreme commander must have a deep insight into the whole condition of the battlefield, the business leader must have insight into the nature of the market he or she confronts, as well as an understanding of the capabilities and likely strategies of the competition. Marlborough's method, as described by Churchill, is one Churchill followed and one that recommends itself to general managers alike:

> The mental process of a general should lead him first to put himself faithfully in the position of the enemy, and to credit that enemy with the readiness to do what he himself would most dread. In the next stage the idiosyncrasies of the hostile commander, the temper and quality of his troops, and the political background come into play. . . . The safe course is to assume that the enemy will do his worst—i.e., what is most unwelcome. With that provided against, lesser evils can be resisted. . . . [Marlborough's] power of putting himself in the enemy's shoes, and measuring truly what they ought to do, and what he himself would most dislike, was one of his greatest gifts. He was only wrong in his anticipations when the enemy made a mistake. But this also had compensations of its own.

Today this anticipation of the strategy of the competition has been formalized into *game theory*. Game theory can be an excellent tool to bring clarity to certain kinds of competitive behavior; for example, price wars among the airlines. Game theorists can point to numerous examples in the business world of strategic decisions that closely parallel the strategic decisions of nations at war. Avinash Dixit of Princeton University and Barry Nalebuff of Yale note that the decision of Polaroid not to diversify beyond the instant photography market, thereby committing itself to a life-or-death battle against any intruders into that market, resembles the decision of Cortés to burn his ships upon his arrival in Mexico in 1519. Just as there would be no turning back and running away from battle for Cortés' army, in a similar fashion, Churchill in 1940 emphatically refused to make any plans to dispatch the British fleet to American ports in the event of Britain's defeat, and he argued against evacuating children to Canada. Both measures, he thought, were "defeatist." Any discussion of transferring the fleet, he wrote, "is bound to weaken confidence here at the moment when all must brace themselves for the supreme struggle." When asked a few days later if the Royal family and certain valuable artworks should be sent to Canada for safety when things looked most bleak, Churchill replied: "None must go. We are going to beat them."

The problem with the quantitative abstractions of game theory, aside from being largely impenetrable to ordinary people, is that the formal models have difficulty quantifying and reliably predicting the irrational element in human motivation and behavior. But what economists and other game theorists would call *irrational behavior* was understood by classical authors to be *passions*, which are much more susceptible to prediction if one pays attention to the character of people. Marlborough, Churchill writes, always "studied attentively the character of his chief opponent." The economists will never understand this essentially intuitive way of thought, or be able to build it into their game theory models, which is one reason few great commanders—or CEOs—have come from the ranks of economists.

Both Marlborough and Churchill displayed command traits that look more like intuition than like rational calculation. Marlborough at times defied the conventional wisdom in his command decisions. Shortly before the battle of Blenheim in August 1704, for example, Marlborough sent the forces of one of his allied commanders, the Margrave of Baden, on a peripheral and secondary attack far from the main field of battle, deliberately weakening Marlborough's overall troop strength to the point of numerical inferiority. Marlborough in fact felt himself stronger without the unreliable troops and inferior generalship of the Margrave. Churchill commented on this unusual decision: "We know of no similar defiance of the sound principle of gathering all forces together for a battle by any of the successful captains of history." Yet Marlborough had the victory.

In the offensive against the Lines of Brabant in Belgium in 1705, Marlborough defied convention again by choosing to attack the enemy's strongest position. "Instead of seeking the weakest part of the defenses," Churchill wrote, "he chose one of the strongest. He argued to himself that because it was the strongest it would be the least considered, and probably defended by the fewest troops. He would feint therefore at the weak part of the lines, and then by a very long night march in the opposite direction his men would assault the earthworks where the defenders were but few." At another occasion Marlborough committed himself to what is always thought the cardinal mistake of military science—dividing his own forces, while at other times he would not even inform his subordinate commanders that their sorties were mere feints rather than the main attack. Just as Churchill in World War II remarked that "truth should be concealed in a bodyguard of lies," Marlborough "made candor serve the purposes of falsehood. . . . He was accustomed by the conditions under which he fought to be continually deceiving friends for their good and foes for their bane."

Observers who were able to discern Churchill's affinity for Marlborough's genius were probably not surprised when in August 1940, at Britain's darkest hour, facing a prospective German invasion that the nation was ill-prepared and underequipped to repulse, Churchill decided to send a significant portion of Britain's tank forces immediately to Cairo, to defend the Suez Canal against a feared Italian offensive, leaving the homeland that much less equipped to meet an invasion. "The decision to give this blood-transfusion while we braced ourselves to meet a mortal danger was at once awful and right," Churchill wrote in his war memoirs.

On the other hand, two months previously, after days of agonizing consideration, Churchill had decided against sending 10 squadrons of fighter planes to France. The French government, desperate in the face of the relentless Nazi drive toward Paris, had pleaded for the fighters. "This decision was one of the hardest to take in the whole war," Sir Ian Jacob, one of Churchill's military advisers, wrote later. "With his great historical sense he felt the urgency of the call from one country to its ally." Churchill went back and forth on the question. His personal sentiment was in favor of sending the planes, because of the moral significance such a gesture would carry for the French, but, significantly, he heeded the cautionary advice of his air minister. "I believe," Jacob wrote, "it was the only occasion in the whole war on which, a firm decision having been reached, the Prime Minister changed his mind. The strain on him must have been almost unbearable." Again, the calculus of Churchill's decision tree was clear in his study of Marlborough:

> Circumstances alone decide whether a correct conventional maneuver is right or wrong. The circumstances include all the factors which are at work at the time; the numbers and quality of the troops and their morale, their weapons, their confidence in their leaders, the character of the country, the condition of the roads, time, and the weather: and behind these the politics of their states. . . . And it is the true comprehension at any given moment of the dynamic sum of all these constantly shifting forces that constitutes military genius.

Churchill knew in June 1940 that the morale of the French army was bad, that battlefield conditions were steadily deteriorating, and finally that the fighter planes would make very little difference while their potential loss in battle would deprive Britain of badly needed protection against the German attack that was sure to follow the fall of France. Here was a case where circumspection had overtaken Churchill's more dominant audacity. Marlborough, Churchill wrote, had "this extraordinary quality of using audacity and circumspection as if they were tools to be picked up and laid down according to the job."

While history is the key to unlocking Churchill's cast of mind, it is a mistake to say he can be explained as a man of the past. The paradox of Churchill is that it was precisely his historical imagination—his insight into the past—that enabled him to be so forward-looking and modern. It is fashionable these days to say that "we live in an age of transition," whether that transition is from an industrial economy to an information economy, or from the modern age to the so-called postmodern age. So deeply ingrained has this cliché become that one expects the Old Testament account of Adam and Eve's expulsion from the Garden of Eden to be rewritten some day so as to have Adam say to Eve, "My dear, we live in an age of transition." But of course so-called historical transitions are only fully obvious after the fact. Everyone *now* understands what the personal computer is doing to change the economy, just as everyone *now* understands how the mass production of the automobile inevitably changed the urban landscape (among other things). Few people understood at the inception of these inventions what the full implications would be. The trick, both for the businessperson confronting the fluid marketplace or the statesman confronting the fluid world scene, is to be able to anticipate what transitions lie ahead, and how best to exploit or control them. Just as a European statesman should consult history to understand the implications of a contemporary change in borders between nations, so too an entrepreneur who wants to understand how a new technology may change the marketplace would do well to study how older technological breakthroughs changed the market—the steam engine, the car, or even the ballpoint pen. Historical imagination, reduced to its essentials, is simply a richer and more colorful form of analogic reasoning.

A person who is purely "of the past" will not be very good at this sort of understanding, which is why Churchill must be excused from the view that his virtue is outmoded or obsolete. On the contrary, Churchill in many ways could be considered the most modern man of the early 20th century. His anticipations of changes to come were uncanny. He wrote about the prospect of nuclear weapons and how they would change warfare—20 years before the first atomic bomb. Three years before the start of World War I, when such a war was still unthinkable to most, Churchill wrote a memorandum predicting in detail how the first 40 days of such a war would unfold. When war came in 1914, the first 40 days went almost exactly according to Churchill's script. He predicted that the Cold War would be resolved in favor of the West; he told his young aide John Colville in 1953—*before* Stalin's death—that if he (Colville) lived his normal span of life, he should assuredly see Eastern Europe free of Communism.

Balancing Overview and Attention to Details

Churchill's penchant for invention and innovation (the subject of Chapter 9), whether the tank or the concrete "mulberry" harbors fashioned for the D-Day invasion, provides a clue to the fourth major key to Churchill's insight, and the necessary complement to his historical imagination and power of decision: He was able to combine a broad understanding of the whole with close attention to detail. Churchill provides a profound example of the golden mean, avoiding equally the pitfalls of grand strategy unsupported by logistics and overwhelming attention to detail in the absence of strategy. In an age obsessed with the idea that the successful executive must delegate to the maximum extent possible, Churchill models a way to resolve the paradox or contradiction of delegating while keeping in close touch with details.

Churchill wrote, "Those who are charged with the direction of supreme affairs must sit on the mountain tops of control; they must never descend into the valleys of direct physical and personal action." Yet early in his premiership—in 1940—Churchill admonished his staff that "an efficient and successful administration manifests itself equally in small as in great matters." In Churchill's case, some of his concerns during his first few weeks as prime minister, when the war crisis was at its worst, ranged from the size of the flag flown outside the Admiralty to whether anyone had inquired as to what care was being taken for the animals in the London zoo during the German air raids. "Churchill scrutinizes every document which has anything to do with the war," one of his private secretaries wrote in his diary, "and does not disdain to enquire into the most trivial point." His concern for details extended even to the code names that were to be used for each military operation. He wanted to be sure they were appropriate for the seriousness of the undertaking. He particularly objected to the proposed code name "Soapsuds" for an operation in the Italian campaign, writing that any operation that might involve significant casualties required a more dignified name. The name was changed to "Tidal Wave."

He was especially worried about food and the rationing regime imposed on British citizens for the duration of the war, and he was always writing with suggestions for how to improve the situation. To the minister of food, who was charged with the difficult task of coping with wartime food scarcities, Churchill inquired: "Have you done justice to rabbit production? Although rabbits are not by themselves nourishing, they are a pretty good mitigation of vegetarianism." Late in the war he sent another message to the minister of food: "On no account reduce the barley for whiskey. This takes years to mature and is an invaluable export and dollar producer. . . . It would be improvident not to preserve this characteristic British element of ascendancy." While at the Admiralty before he became prime minister, Churchill worried that the requisitioning of small ships from the fishing fleets would diminish the fish catch. Churchill circulated a memo calling for attention to this problem and a policy of "utmost fish." Later in the war he issued a memorandum to military commanders to ensure that soldiers on the front lines received beer rations "before any of the parties in the rear get a drop."

His interest in detail was related to his strong intellectual curiosity. He insisted on having the mechanics and theory of every new invention explained to him, from radar to magnetic mines to early rockets. He gave constant encouragement to inventors. He had immediately grasped the significance of the airplane when he first heard of its invention, writing from the Board of Trade in 1910 that he thought Britain should get in touch with the Wright brothers at once. He would quickly appreciate how a new invention or innovation to an old device could be best used, and he would issue lengthy memoranda about their proper use. For example, he was closely involved with the development of countermeasures for the magnetic mine, which the Germans deployed with great effect in the early days of the war, and he was quick to promote the use of countermeasures once they were developed. It was also his idea to drop tin foil strips from bombers to confuse enemy radar.

Again, it was his historical imagination, which by necessity is fueled with the study of detail, that enabled Churchill to range across the large mass of detail that confronts a war leader. John Winant, the American Ambassador to England in 1941, wrote that "There was no detail of the problem before us which was not alive to him and on which his knowledge of the past did not throw light as well as constructive criticism."

The chapters that follow will take up these aspects of Churchill's character, intellect, and imagination, along with many subsidiary but important aspects of his leadership, and explore them in detail.

KEYS TO UNDERSTANDING CHURCHILL

• *Candor and plain speaking.*
Churchill's maxim: "I have often had to eat my words, and I must confess that I have always found it a wholesome diet."

• *Decisiveness. Churchill liked to deliberate and make firm decisions.*
Churchill's maxims: "Ponder, and then *act*." "An accepted leader has only to be sure of what it is best to do, or at least to have made up his mind about it."

• *Historical imagination.*
Churchill's maxim: "The longer you look back, the farther you can look forward."

• *The ability to balance a view of the whole scene with attention to details.*
Churchill's maxim: "An efficient and successful administration manifests itself equally in small as in great matters."

CHAPTER 2

THE EXECUTIVE CHURCHILL

A Brief Survey of His Career in Public Office

———◆———

Curse ruthless time! Curse our mortality! How cruelly short is the allotted span for all we must cram into it! We are all worms. But I do believe that I am a glow worm.
— WINSTON S. CHURCHILL, 1907

I T I S N O T immediately obvious, even when reading one of the Churchill biographies, how extensive was Churchill's executive experience. Precisely because it was so extensive, you tend to lose the forest for the trees while the more colorful aspects of Churchill's life and character come to the forefront. Between 1907 and 1940, Churchill served in seven different cabinet posts, and one subcabinet post, in addition to being prime minister. He began his ministerial career as one of the youngest men ever to serve in high office, and he ended his career as one of the oldest prime ministers in British history. The only major cabinet post he never held was foreign secretary—and he was seriously considered for that job on one occasion. The course of these posts saw Churchill experience glittering triumphs that would seem to propel him shortly to the premiership, and shattering setbacks from which it seemed unlikely that he could ever recover.

In addition to his government service, Churchill served as a director of several different private companies, and nearly managed the merger of two large oil companies until his recall back to government service caused him to have to give up the project. Finally, Churchill can also be considered an entrepreneur and an investor: throughout his life he earned most of his income from writing. He wrote countless short articles for newspapers and magazines, and his large book projects required him to retain and manage a research and secretarial staff, which he referred to at one point as his "syndicate." He invested his earnings heavily in the stock market with mixed results; he was wiped out on more than one occasion. Late in life he even enjoyed some success as a racehorse owner. A brief outline of these various offices and experiences and the issues and controversies they involved will clarify the manifold aspects of Churchill's leadership to be explored in the chapters ahead.

Table 1 displays Churchill's major offices, the most significant initiatives or concerns of each office, and the record of success or failure with each issue. (The Appendix provides additional details about these offices and Churchill's accomplishments, and readers unfamiliar with the entire Churchill story may find it useful to review that before proceeding with the main text.) As the table shows, Churchill enjoyed more successes than failures, but the few initiatives that did miscarry were of sufficient scale to cost him dearly. But in every post Churchill displayed his signature leadership traits, especially his penchant for organizational innovation and refinement.

Churchill's executive career divides neatly into two distinct phases. Early in his ministerial career, as president of the Board of Trade and as home secretary (these posts are roughly equivalent to the American cabinet posts of secretary of commerce, secretary of labor, and attorney general), Churchill was concerned mostly with domestic affairs. During these years Churchill was a liberal reformer, one of the architects of the British welfare state.

Starting in 1911 with his appointment as First Lord of the Admiralty (equivalent to the U.S. secretary of the Navy), Churchill's career was henceforth to be devoted mostly to foreign and military affairs. This suited both his education—he had been a cadet at Sandhurst, a British military academy—and his youthful experience as a soldier and war correspondent, where he won the fame that launched his political career. (Several of the chapters that follow

TABLE 1   CHURCHILL'S EXECUTIVE CAREER

EXECUTIVE OFFICE	MAJOR INITIATIVES	RESULT
Colonial Under-Secretary (1905–1908)	Transvaal constitution	Success
President, Board of Trade (1908–1910)	Labor dispute mediation	Success
	Arbitration courts	Mixed
	Labor exchanges	Success
	Minimum wage	Success
Home Secretary (1910–1911)	Strike intervention	Mixed
	Home rule for Ireland	Inconclusive
	Prison reform	Mixed
	Insurance Act	Success
	Labor and Shop Acts	Success
First Lord of the Admiralty (1911–1915)	Naval staff reorganization	Success
	Fleet power conversion (coal to oil)	Success
	Naval Air Corps	Success
	Ship development project	Success
	Tank development project	Success
	Dardanelles offensive	Failure
Minister of Munitions (1917–1919)	Streamlining of ministry	Success
	Output increases	Success
Secretary of State for Air & War (1919–1920)	Russian intervention	Failure
	Demobilization	Success
Colonial Secretary (1920–1922)	Home rule for Ireland	Mixed
	Middle East reorganization	Success
Chancellor of the Exchequer (1924–1929)	Gold standard restoration	Failure
	Income tax reduction	Success
	Sweeping tax reform	Failure
	Coal strike mediation	Failure
First Lord of the Admiralty (1939–1940)	Norwegian offensive	Failure
Prime Minister (1940–1945)	World War II	Success
Prime Minister (1951–1955)	Cold War settlement mediation	Failure

discuss his accomplishments and setbacks at the Admiralty as they apply to the chapter themes.)

As Churchill climbed the executive ladder of the British government, he displayed two traits worthy of emulation by other executives rising in an organizational hierarchy. The first is that he set out in nearly every case not only to *learn* how the new office operated but also to *define the job* in broad new ways. It "had always been his custom on entering a new ministry," Martin Gilbert wrote, to submit his new subordinate staff officials to "a barrage of written questions, in which he sought both to find out about the routine of departmental business, and to set the tone for his own policies." He always defined the broad vistas of his job in relation to the whole of the government, and how his department could help make the government a success. "I want this government not to fritter away its energies on all sorts of small schemes," he remarked early in his tenure at the Treasury. "I want them to concentrate on one or two things which will be big land-marks in the history of this Parliament."

This inclination for the large initiative meant, second, that in every ministry he led, Churchill was not content simply to manage the department in a business-as-usual manner. Churchill was never content to be, as he once wrote in a different context, "the passive matrix upon which others impose their plans." Most instructive is a letter written to Prime Minister Baldwin toward the end of Churchill's tenure as chancellor of the exchequer in 1928, when the idea of a sweeping tax-reform scheme was germinating in his mind. He had already passed an income tax cut and had several other large accomplishments as chancellor. But, as he wrote to Baldwin, there is "the great need we have to dominate events lest we be submerged by them. Each year it is necessary for a modern British Government to place some large issue or measure before the country, or to be engaged in some public struggle which holds the public mind." After reviewing past successful and unsuccessful measures as a way of showing that this was no time for the government to rest on its laurels, Churchill continued: "It is for these reasons that I have been casting about for some large new constructive measure which, by its importance and scope, by its antagonisms as well as by its appeal, will lift us above the ruck of current affairs."

To put it in simple terms that verge on cliché, the leader is always striving to conceive and implement new initiatives without which no purposeful organization can maintain its momentum. Churchill was relentless in his drive for mastery of affairs. These inclinations served him well at the moment of supreme trial in World War II.

CHURCHILL LESSONS

• *It is not enough simply to learn the job: Define it.*
Churchill's maxim: Do not become the passive matrix upon which others impose their designs.

• *Always look for opportunities to advance bold new initiatives.*
Churchill's maxim: Do not fritter away your energy on small schemes.

CHAPTER 3

CONFRONTING FAILURE AND LEARNING FROM MISTAKES

We must learn from misfortune the means of future strength.
—WINSTON S. CHURCHILL, 1938

AVOIDING RISKS IN business is the route to failure. Avoiding risks in politics, however, is the route to a long career in office. A failed risk in politics is far more dangerous than a failed risk in business. In business, shareholders and customers will quickly forgive you if you recover from a disaster—think of Coca-Cola after the "New Coke" debacle, or Ford after the Edsel. But in politics, partisans will keep alive and distort and magnify any failure or mistake in your career. Often small mistakes are punished more severely than disasters. Churchill observed: "In all great business very large errors are excused or even unperceived, but in definite and local matters small mistakes are punished out of all proportion." This is one reason politicians are risk-averse, and why modern government administration seeks to minimize risk and avoid failure through a mindless bureaucratic process that delivers mostly mediocrity. Churchill's refusal throughout his career to practice bland, risk-averse politics stands out as his most striking leadership attribute. Churchill's audacious and risk-taking character was at the core of his genius, but also constituted the chief liability of his long career and nearly led to his ruin. The lessons he learned from the mistakes and setbacks early in his career proved instrumental in his future success as war leader in World War II.

"Politics are almost as exciting as war and quite as dangerous," Churchill once wrote. "In war you can only be killed once, but in politics many times." But there was never a moment of doubt in his mind that great risks must be taken. He never flinched at the possibility of failure. Churchill understood that without great risks, no great achievements were possible. "*He takes huge risks*," one of his leading contemporaries wrote emphatically of him. It may have been in his genes. His illustrious ancestor, the Duke of Marlborough, had undertaken huge risks with the continental army in the European wars of the 18th century. The duke emerged triumphant in war, but defeated in politics back home. Churchill's father, Lord Randolph Churchill (whose own political career came to a crashing end on account of a miscalculated risk), once described Benjamin Disraeli's career as "Failure, failure, failure, partial success, renewed failure, ultimate and complete triumph." It is a description that applies in some respects to Winston. Churchill himself once quipped that "success is going from failure to failure without loss of enthusiasm"—a worthy credo for an entrepreneur.

Like any bold risk-taker, Churchill had his share of failures and debacles—for many of which he does not deserve the complete blame. Nevertheless, at several points in his long career he himself thought he might not recover. "I am finished," he said upon being ousted from the government in 1915. His enemies and critics were even more eager to pounce on his mistakes and pronounce his permanent demise. Decades after the First World War, hecklers would shout "What about the Dardanelles?" during his public speeches— a reference to the military fiasco in Turkey that had become known as "Churchill's Folly." When, during Lady Astor's visit to the Soviet Union in 1937, Joseph Stalin asked her about Churchill's prospects, she replied, "Churchill? Oh, he's *finished*." At about this same time a friend wrote that Churchill's life had become "a quagmire from which there seemed to be no rescue." One of the leading studies of

Churchill's pre–World War II years bears the subtitle, "A Study in Failure."

Throughout his life, Churchill's critics spread the view that he was reckless, even dangerous and perhaps unstable, and certainly lacking in judgment. These estimates of Churchill's character and acumen derived largely from his bitter experience in World War I, and from the fact that most of his contemporaries had failed to absorb the same lessons of the war that Churchill did. World War I offers a classic case study in poor decision making and organizational confusion, and also how a person of imagination and resolve can go wrong in the midst of such a situation when confined to a subordinate position. As First Lord of the Admiralty during the first year of World War I, Churchill had a front-row seat for what he regarded as an unrelenting spectacle of incompetence, fractured decision making, and drift.

Churchill's own initiatives, and those he urged upon his colleagues in the government, would eventually cost him his place in the government and attach a permanent stain to his reputation. The mistakes and lessons of World War I—especially his own—were constantly on Churchill's mind throughout World War II. (Churchill was the only member of the war cabinet in World War II who had been in the war cabinet during World War I.) Neither he nor the government he led in the later war would make those same mistakes.

There were three major failings of the administration of World War I. First, Britain's war deliberations were mired in confusion from the outset, owing chiefly to a lack of strong, decisive leadership at the top; second, there was poor understanding of how new battlefield conditions favoring the defensive had created a costly stalemate; third, there was a lack of strategic imagination about ways to break out of this stalemate. These latter two failings were closely related to the first—the failure of leadership at the top.

Confusion at the Top

Churchill remarked during World War II that most strategic failure in war owed to "the total absence of one directing mind and commanding willpower." In Britain, grand strategy was the responsibility of the war cabinet, but ultimately the war cabinet required the direction and prodding of the prime minister. Prime Minister Herbert Asquith was simply not up to the task. It was not only that his passive management style was unsuited to the active requirements of making war; he was frankly bored with the details of conducting warfare. "We had a long Cabinet this morning," Asquith wrote a confidant before the war was even a month old, "mostly about rather boring details connected with the war." Two weeks later Asquith wrote again: "We had a Cabinet this morning—a mass of details, but nothing really interesting."

Asquith was what we would call in today's jargon a *passive-aggressive* leader. His preferred method of management was to let his subordinates thrash out their differences and settle disagreements among themselves, with a minimum of direct intervention from him. One of Asquith's favorite maxims was "wait and see." Churchill's description of how Asquith conducted cabinet business is illuminating:

> In Cabinet he was markedly silent. Indeed he never spoke a word in Council if he could get his way without it. He sat, like the great Judge he was, hearing with trained patience the case deployed on every side, now and then interjecting a question or brief comment, searching or pregnant, which gave matters a turn towards the goal he wished to reach; and when at the end, amid all the perplexities and cross-currents of ably and vehemently expressed opinion, he summed up, it was very rarely that the silence he had observed till then, did not fall on all.

This may be a suitable and effective method of organizational leadership for peacetime politics, but it was disastrous once World War I began. It is for these reasons that the British writer Rebecca West suggested that Asquith would have made an excellent butler.

Asquith's war council, which met infrequently, had trouble reaching firm decisions, and often reversed those decisions at subsequent meetings. This left the direction of the war almost wholly in the hands of military commanders, whose stubborn strategy of attrition was already leading to frightful casualties. Churchill quickly grew disenchanted with Asquith, whose peacetime leadership he had greatly admired. Before the war was even four months old a worried Churchill wrote to Asquith: "We ought not to drift. . . . Without your direct guidance and initiative, none of these things will be done; and a succession of bloody checks in the West and in the East will leave the allies dashed in spirit and bankrupt in policy." A few weeks later Churchill urged Asquith to hold war council meetings more frequently: "I think the War Council ought to meet daily for a few days next week. No topic can be pursued to any fruitful result at weekly intervals."

Churchill's admonitions proved unavailing. A year later, after Churchill had been removed from the Admiralty, a new cabinet colleague wrote to him in exasperation: "all our calculations (if we can dignify them by that name) are absolutely haphazard. . . . I have not yet been at any Cabinet when anything was properly or usefully decided. . . . Surely outside a Cabinet such delay and want of policy would not be tolerated in any business." For months Churchill had been complaining that "nowhere has there been design and decision . . . without decision and design very terrible catastrophe may ensue." As the drift continued, Churchill's comments were growing more acerbic: "The numbing hand of Asquith is over everything, and all initiative and energy seem paralyzed." "History will hold a strict account of every day's indecision," he sternly warned.

Misunderstanding the Implications of Technology

The second major failing of World War I was the lack of appreciation of how the state of modern warfare would lead to a costly stalemate. Except for Churchill, there was little imagination for changing these circumstances. New technologies have always led to radical changes in the conduct of warfare, and have tipped the advantage back and forth between offense and defense. Over the centuries, innovations such as the longbow, mounted cavalry, and the cannon provided new advantages to offensive warfare, and helped offensive armies overcome defenses such as castles and similar fortifications. By contrast, in World War I the machine gun, mortar, and trench provided a significant advantage to the defensive position. Each attack on the Western Front in World War I left the attacking force weaker. "Are there not other alternatives than sending our armies to chew barbed wire in Flanders?" Churchill asked after just a few weeks of war.

"The mechanical danger must be overcome by a mechanical remedy," Churchill wrote in a long memo on the issue, "Mechanical Power in the Offensive." Chapter 9 recounts the history of Churchill's sponsorship of the tank, but the tank was not his only idea for an invention that would make battlefield offensives less costly. He proposed the development of armor plating, mechanical trench diggers, and trench-spanning machines. He pushed the idea of using smoke to shroud the battlefield. But the tank would be slow in coming, and his other ideas either did not come to fruition or were insufficient to the scale of the problem. So he also pushed against the third major failing of wartime leadership: grand strategy.

Failures of Strategy

In his book on World War I, *The World Crisis*, Churchill observed:

Battles are won by slaughter and maneuver. The greater the
general, the more he contributes in maneuver, the less he
demands in slaughter. . . . There is required for the composition
of the great commander not only massive common sense and
reasoning power, not only imagination, but also an element of
legerdemain, an original and sinister touch, which leaves the
enemy puzzled as well as beaten . . . the object of all is to find
easier ways, other than sheer slaughter, of achieving the
main purpose.

With trenches running from the North Sea to the Swiss Alps,
there were no flanks to be turned, no room for strategic maneuver.
Seeing that the stalemate along the trenches of the Western Front in
France could not be broken, Churchill realized that the only way
to break the stalemate would be to open a new front somewhere.
Like a manufacturer trying to outflank competitors through a different product specialty rather than through direct price competition, Churchill realized that victory might come far away from the
main field of battle. "The decisive theater is the theater where a
vital decision may be obtained at any time," Churchill wrote. "The
main theater is that in which the main armies or fleets are stationed.
This is not at all times the decisive theater."

With his genius for comprehending the whole scene, Churchill
cast his gaze to the distant shores of the Eastern Mediterranean.
Turkey had entered the war on the side of Germany, which added
considerable pressure against Russia on the Eastern Front. If pressure could somehow be brought against Turkey, or, even better, if
Turkey could be knocked out of the war entirely, it would change the
entire complexion of the war. It would relieve German pressure on
Russia and perhaps even prompt Greece and one or two of the other
Balkan countries to join the war on the side of allies. Italy might
even join, which would be the greatest boon. But how was this to
be done? Where were the resources to be found? The huge manpower needs of the Western Front in France, as well as the purely

defensive needs for British colonial possessions in Palestine, Egypt, and India, made it impossible to contemplate a full-scale offensive against Turkey. The troops and weaponry were simply unavailable on a sufficient scale. So Churchill looked for an alternative.

The linchpin of Turkey was its ancient capital city, Constantinople (nowadays known as Istanbul). Constantinople sits near the junction of the Black Sea and nature's most remarkable natural canal, the Bosporus, which connects the Black Sea with the Aegean Sea. The narrowest part of the strait, near the Aegean entrance to the waterway, is known as the Dardanelles, bordered on one side by the Gallipoli peninsula—regarded as the end of Europe, and the other side by Asia Minor—Turkey, the beginning of Asia. Just as a surprise attack on Pearl Harbor had been a theoretical exercise for Japanese naval officers for many years before December 7, 1941, the possibility of a purely naval expedition against Constantinople, which would involve forcing the narrow straits of the Dardanelles with a substantial fleet and bombarding fixed fortifications on the high cliffs above the straits, had been contemplated as a theoretical exercise by the British navy throughout the 19th century. With the advance of larger and more accurate modern howitzers, it had become the conventional wisdom that from about the 1880s onward a naval attack past the Dardanelles fortresses was no longer possible. Churchill himself had written in 1911: "It is no longer possible to force the Dardanelles . . . nobody would expose a modern fleet to such perils."

But Churchill wondered. Knowing of the advances both in armor plating for modern warships and in the accuracy of their newer and larger guns, in early January 1915 (five months into the war) he inquired of Admiral Carden, the commander of the fleet in the eastern Mediterranean, whether he thought it possible to force the Dardanelles "by ships alone." Admiral Carden's reply electrified Churchill and the other members of the British war cabinet: "They [the Dardanelles] might be forced by extended operations with a large number of ships." One thing England enjoyed was "a large number of ships," especially older battleships that were scheduled soon for the scrap heap, and therefore expendable on a promising risk. The naval losses from the proposed action would be small compared to the losses the armies in France were incurring day after day.

The naval attack commenced in February and reached a climax on March 18, 1915, with encouraging signs that success might soon follow. Constantinople, which would be virtually defenseless from naval bombardment once ships cleared the straits, was gripped with panic, and the Turkish government prepared to flee the city. All Europe held its breath in anticipation. "The effects of the naval operation were electrical," Churchill wrote. It looked like his strategic idea would be a triumph, and perhaps speed the war to an early conclusion.

Anyone who has seen the early Mel Gibson film, *Gallipoli*, will know that the operation ended up with the same kind of trench warfare and appalling slaughter that characterized the Western Front. The British eventually withdrew from Gallipoli eight months later, after suffering enormous losses. The Dardanelles became synonymous with fiasco and recklessness. It was this outcome that dogged Churchill for the rest of his life, and still clouds his reputation today. Australia's official military historian, C.E.W. Bean, wrote, "Through the fatal power of a young enthusiast to convince older and slower brains, the tragedy of Gallipoli was born." British historian Robert Rhodes James, in a paraphrase of Churchill's own ill-chosen words about the matter, wrote that the Dardanelles offensive was a "wholly illegitimate war gamble."

What went wrong? How did a purely naval operation with such promise and signs of early success turn into another exercise in "chewing barbed wire"?

Historians and military experts will argue forever about whether the Dardanelles idea was sound or about whether it was properly executed by the naval commanders on the spot. From an executive management point of view, however, it is clear that the whole enterprise was afflicted from beginning to end with indecision, divided counsel, conflicting orders, and second-guessing. The war council met 15 times on this issue between November 1914 and mid-March 1915, when the initial plan for a purely naval attack was abandoned in favor of an amphibious landing. Throughout this series of meetings, the war council went back and forth about whether to commit to a purely naval attack ("by ships alone") or whether to mount a combined offensive with an amphibious landing of army troops on the Gallipoli peninsula to back up the naval attack. At the first meeting where the idea was discussed, on November 25, 1914 (just four months into the war), Churchill had favored the idea of a combined operation. Churchill's First Sea Lord, Lord Fisher, was enthusiastically in favor of a combined attack on Turkey. However, both Prime Minister Asquith and Lord Herbert Kitchener, who, as secretary of state for war, headed the army, opposed the idea. Kitchener said there were no troops available for such an operation. Kitchener suggested to Churchill a few days later that perhaps a naval "demonstration" could be made against the Turkish forts. This, in part, prompted Churchill's query to Admiral Carden about whether an attack "by ships alone" might be able to get through.

For the next two meetings, the war council seemed to be heading toward a commitment for the purely naval attack, which had the virtue of being able to be discontinued immediately and at relatively little cost if it proved unsuccessful. But then in the fourth meeting, Lord Kitchener seemed to change his mind, suggesting that 150,000 troops might be found for an invasion at the Dardanelles. He had not, however, studied the idea with any thoroughness. Five days later, Kitchener changed his mind again and said that no troops were available. At the sixth meeting of the war council two weeks after that, Kitchener further confused the deliberations by suggesting that the reserve 29th Division might be available for an offensive in the eastern theater, but at Salonica (on the Turkish mainland) and not at the Dardanelles. Meanwhile First Sea Lord Fisher was changing his mind on the subject, first opposing the purely naval attack, and then later adopting the idea "whole hog—*totus porcus*," as he

put it. (He would later change his mind back again, and his resignation would set in motion the chain of events that led to Churchill's
ouster from the Admiralty.) Over the course of the next three war
council meetings, the decision was tentatively made to send the
29th Division to the Dardanelles for a combined operation. "You get
through [with the navy]," Kitchener told Churchill, "I will find the
men." Then, at the next war council meeting just three days later,
Kitchener changed his mind yet again, and said the 29th Division
was not available. For this and the next two meetings the war council argued back and forth, with Churchill and others pleading with
Kitchener for the troops. Each meeting postponed a decision about
the 29th Division until a further meeting. During this interlude,
Kitchener canceled transport preparations for the 29th Division
without informing Churchill, whose responsibility it was to oversee
the operation. Finally, at the 13th meeting of the war council on
March 10, Kitchener agreed to release the 29th Division for the Dardanelles. But this was barely a week before the naval attack was to be
launched, and no plans had been made for landing the troops.

Amid this indecision and divided counsel, it is not surprising that
the naval commanders on the spot lost their nerve when the attack
of March 18 resulted in heavy losses. (Churchill came to refer to
Admiral De Robeck, the commander of the fleet on the scene, as
"De *Rowback*.") Even though intelligence at the time (which was
subsequently confirmed as accurate) suggested that the naval
attack came within a hair of success, and that an immediately
renewed attack would almost surely succeed with minimal further
loss, the naval attack was broken off to await the arrival of the army
almost a month later. Churchill had wanted to press on with the
naval attack, but lacked the authority to decide the matter. The naval
operation would give way to an army invasion and therefore pass
largely out of Churchill's ambit. But this would take more than a
month to set in motion. By this time British intentions were trans-
parent, and the delay enabled the Turks to reinforce the Gallipoli
peninsula, thus setting the stage for another costly trench warfare

stalemate. A quicker decision about the idea might have changed everything. Instead, the Allies suffered 252,000 casualties at Gallipoli over the next eight futile months. Throughout the summer and fall the war council was indecisive and tentative about whether to end the operation, going back and forth once again about whether to continue or end the operation. "The Dardanelles has run on like a Greek tragedy," Churchill wrote several months after.

The unfolding disaster was becoming evident in May 1915 when, as a result of a growing political crisis, Churchill was dismissed from the Admiralty and a new coalition government under Asquith was formed. Even though the Dardanelles idea had not been his alone, Churchill quickly became the scapegoat for the debacle. "History will vindicate the conception and the errors in execution will on the whole leave me clear," he wrote.

Learning from Disaster

The lessons of the Dardanelles were immediately apparent to Churchill. "Nothing leads more surely to disaster," he wrote to David Lloyd-George, "than that a military plan should be pursued with crippled steps and in a lukewarm spirit in the face of continual nagging within the executive circle. United ought not to mean that a number of gentlemen are willing to sit together on condition either that the evil day of decision is postponed, or that not more than a half-decision should be provisionally adopted. Even in politics such methods are unhealthy. In war they are a crime." (The Dardanelles campaign was only one of many issues about which the war council could not reach clear and consistent decisions. The war council deliberated on the issue of conscription in at least 12 meetings without reaching a decision.)

The most important lesson Churchill learned from the management and direction of World War I is that *responsibility must be combined with authority*. Churchill realized that it was a mistake that prepared the way for failure to take on responsibility without having complete authority, whether it was for the development and deployment of a new weapon like the tank, or for a far more sweeping strategic initiative such as the Dardanelles. In *The River War*, Churchill had written that "few sensations are more painful than responsibility without power." Now he had experienced this firsthand. The unraveling of the Dardanelles operations taught him that it is a mistake "to carry out a major and cardinal operation of war from a subordinate position." "My one fatal mistake," he wrote on another occasion, "was trying to achieve a great enterprise without having the plenary authority which could so easily have carried it to success."

It was in memory of these confused counsels that when Churchill became prime minister in World War II, he decided to be his own defense minister, rather than appointing someone to oversee war plans. This way he kept close control of the strategic direction of the war. He held all the reins in his hands, so to speak, and could press for firm decision. Some degree of collective decision making is necessary in all large-scale enterprises, but any form of collective decision making, in the absence of a single dominating mind at the top, is prone to temporizing. In World War II, Churchill remarked that the chiefs-of-staff system "leads to weak and faltering decisions—or rather indecisions. Why, when you take the most gallant sailor, the most intrepid airman, or the most audacious soldier, put them at a table together—what do you get? The sum total of their fears!" On the contrary, Churchill thought, "every war decision must be forced to a clear-cut issue. . . . The soldiers ordered to their deaths have a right to a plan, as well as a cause." The failure to reach firm decisions, he thought, was the result of "the want of drive of the man in charge." The man at the top "must continually drive the vast machine forward at its utmost speed. To lose momentum is not merely to stop, but to fall." Above all, Churchill stressed throughout World War II, "Whatever course was decided upon, it was essential that we should now act decisively."

Churchill was to make sure that the sorry state of affairs of World War I did not occur in World War II. On several occasions when his leadership and consolidation of power came under criticism in the House of Commons during World War II, Churchill invariably replied: "What you have no right to do is to ask me to bear responsibilities without the power of effective action."

The Dardanelles catastrophe led Churchill to lay out what he called "the five distinct truths" governing decisions about military operations, five principles that can apply equally well to business leadership and decision making:

1. That there is full authority.
2. That there is a reasonable prospect of success.
3. That greater interests are not compromised.
4. That all possible care and forethought are exercised in the preparation.
5. That all vigor and determination are shown in the execution.

The Dardanelles operation failed the first and the last test, but even if Churchill had possessed more authority and even had the commanders on the scene not lost their nerve, it might still have failed. Yet the defeat of a military operation does not in itself disprove the soundness of the concept. While Churchill rued the outcome and unfairly suffered the major blame for the Dardanelles fiasco, it did not cause him to shrink from risks in the future. "It is not right," Churchill wrote in 1916, "to condemn operations of war simply because they involve risk and uncertainty. Some operations can and ought to be made certainties. Others belong to the class where one can only balance the chances, and action must proceed on a preponderance of favorable chances."

The essential strategic soundness of the Dardanelles offensive has come to be more deeply appreciated as the decades have passed. Basil Liddell-Hart, one of Britain's leading military historians, described the Dardanelles as "a sound and far-sighted conception, marred by a chain of errors in execution almost unrivaled even in British history." It presents one of the great what-ifs of history. Had Turkey been knocked out early and the war ended sooner, perhaps the Bolshevik revolution would never have taken place. Perhaps Hitler would never have risen to power. These kinds of questions can never be answered, and it is perhaps frivolous even to indulge them. But it is a tribute to Churchill's insight that nearly 50 years after the episode, Clement Attlee, who was Churchill's great opponent (it was Attlee and the Labour Party who defeated Churchill in the election of 1945), remarked to Churchill that the Dardanelles operation was "the only imaginative strategic idea of the war. I only wish that you had had full power to carry it to success."

THE LESSONS OF FAILURE

- *Responsibility must be combined with authority.*
Churchill's maxims: "My one fatal mistake was trying to achieve a great enterprise without having the plenary authority which could so easily have carried it to success." "What you have no right to do is to ask me to bear responsibilities without the power of effective action."

- *Decisiveness depends on the person at the top.*
Churchill's maxims: "Every decision must be forced to a clear-cut issue." "You must continually drive the vast machine forward at its utmost speed. To lose momentum is not merely to stop, but to fall."

CHAPTER 4

CHURCHILL ON ADMINISTRATION

Responsibility and Organization

———◆———

There ought to be ways of reforming a business, other than by merely putting more money into it.

—WINSTON S. CHURCHILL, 1901

Despite Churchill's extensive executive experience and his success at the summit of leadership in World War II, he oddly gained the reputation—both among his contemporaries and among many subsequent historians—as a poor administrator. "Churchill himself was no administrator," wrote John Colville, one of his parliamentary secretaries when he was prime minister. Historian Robert Rhodes James argues "that administration was not to be numbered among Churchill's ministerial qualities."

These opinions are surely wrong. Martin Gilbert writes in his massive biography, "Churchill's colleagues and subordinates were much impressed by his administrative skills. On 17 July 1917 Christopher Addison noted in his diary: 'There is no more capable chief of a department than he is.'" Churchill's office during World War II, Gilbert adds, was "a model of efficiency at times of unprecedented danger." Military historian Maxwell Schoenfeld wrote that "Churchill was an administrative colossus." And Isaiah Berlin observed that "his personal private office was run in a sharply disciplined manner. His habits, though unusual, were regular." The misperception of Churchill's executive style arises from a fact that has been noted previously: his style did not comport well in a system of politics that purposely diffuses responsibility and clarity. As Isaiah Berlin observed of Churchill: "No strongly centralized political organization feels altogether happy with individuals who combine independence, a free imagination, and a formidable strength of character with a stubborn faith and a single-minded, unchanging view of the public and private good." So while Churchill may have been something of a square peg in the round hole of ordinary peacetime politics, the conditions of war demanded the kind of sharper focus and decisive edge that he had to offer. These skills are more like the kind required of executives in the competitive commercial marketplace. As a result, Churchill's example is actually more useful to people in private industry than to politicians.

Churchill's administrative principles and practices had one dominant, unifying purpose: to facilitate clear decisions and enable prompt, efficient execution of those decisions. "The efficiency of a war Administration," he wrote in his war memoirs, "depends mainly upon whether decisions emanating from the highest approved authority are in fact strictly, faithfully, and punctually obeyed." He employed a large number of distinctive habits, practices and character traits to achieve this end, which will be explored in detail over the next three chapters. This chapter concentrates on the cardinal habits and executive strategies he employed throughout his career:

- Take charge and assume full responsibility.
- Use a simplified organizational structure that emphasizes responsibility.

These habits may sound banal to the point of cliché, yet in example after example it will be seen that Churchill was effective in contrast to his predecessors and colleagues precisely to the extent that they did not practice these habits in sufficient degree.

Taking Charge and Assuming Responsibility

We often praise a take-charge kind of person, but asserting one's leadership comes along with the obligation to assume responsibility for the outcome of whatever events are set in motion. Churchill understood both sides of this coin from a very early age. "Churchill always liked to take the lead in any matter in which he was concerned," his son Randolph wrote.

Chapter 1 quoted the remark that Churchill is the kind of person to consult if you wanted a mountain moved. Though Churchill never moved a mountain, he did once move a small river, during his schooldays as a young cadet at Sandhurst. He dropped a gold watch his father had given him into a deep pool in a stream. Despite attempts to dive to the bottom of the pool, he was unable to retrieve the watch. Dredging was equally unsuccessful. So Churchill hired 23 soldiers from a nearby infantry detachment (reportedly at a cost of £3, not an inconsiderable sum in 1893) to dig a new channel for the river, after which Churchill procured a fire engine to pump out the pool. The watch was recovered.

This kind of pattern can be seen throughout Churchill's life. If something needed doing, he didn't wait for any collective council to shuffle their feet and clear their throats and persuade someone to lead the effort. Churchill always stepped forward, even if unasked. One weekend in 1908 when Churchill was staying at Burley-on-the-Hill, a country estate, a serious fire broke out in the middle of the night. Churchill's private secretary, Eddie Marsh, recorded that "Winston commandeered a fireman's helmet and assumed the direction of operations."

One of the most notorious examples of Churchill taking charge was the famous "Siege of Sidney Street" in 1910, when Churchill was home secretary. A gang of burglars who had shot and killed three London policemen were tracked down to a house on Sidney Street in London's East End. The burglars (who were actually part of an immigrant anarchist gang) were heavily armed and overmatched the lightly armed London police. Churchill authorized the dispatch of a detachment of Scots Guards from the Tower of London. But as there was little information about what was going on at the scene,

Churchill decided—"characteristically," his son Randolph wrote—
to go to the scene himself. He did not intervene in the actual conduct
of the siege, but soon the house caught fire, and when the fire
brigade arrived, Churchill made a decision. Believing that firemen
would be in danger of being shot if they approached the building, he
ordered the fire brigade to stand fast. "I thought it better to let
the house burn down than spend good British lives in rescuing those
ferocious rascals," he later wrote. When a fire brigade officer sought
to confirm this order, Churchill replied: "Quite right; I accept full
responsibility." The burglars never surrendered, and after the building burned to the ground, their bodies were found inside. A photo of
Churchill at the scene appeared in the newspapers, and caused a
controversy. His critics thought he had gone to the scene just to be
a publicity hound, and had interfered with the police command on
the spot. (He hadn't.) Churchill later reflected that he probably
shouldn't have yielded to his "curiosity."

The defense of Antwerp in the early weeks of World War I is a
more dramatic example. As the right wing of the German invasion
swept through Belgium in the first few weeks of the war, it appeared
as though the Belgian army would crumble and leave northwestern
France vulnerable. The British Expeditionary Force had not yet
established itself sufficiently on this part of the front. Above all, it
was imperative to the defense of Britain that the key channel ports
be kept in Allied hands. (This was the phase of the war known as
"the race to the sea.") The early capitulation of Belgium would
probably lead to the German capture of the channel ports. The city
of Antwerp, key to the region, was under heavy German attack. If
Antwerp could hold out, the situation could be rescued.

The cabinet decided to send Churchill to Belgium. Prime Minister Asquith wrote to a confidant about Churchill's mission: "I don't
know how fluent he is in French, but if he is able to do himself justice in a foreign tongue, the Belges will have listened to a discourse
the like of which they have never heard before. I cannot but think

that he will stiffen them up to the sticking point." But the situation at Antwerp was worse than they had imagined. Churchill found the Belgians "weary and disheartened." Churchill succeeded in temporarily bucking up the Belgians ("Under Winston's stimulus the Belgians are making a resolute stand," Asquith wrote), but he could see that it was an eroding situation. Even though Churchill had pressing duties back at the Admiralty, "he had come to believe," Martin Gilbert wrote, "that Antwerp's continued resistance depended to a large extent upon his remaining in the city." Churchill then took "the extraordinary step," as Gilbert wrote, of offering to resign from the cabinet and take formal command of military forces in the field. This offer was greeted with "a Homeric laugh" by his cabinet colleagues, except for General Herbert Kitchener (secretary of state for war in the cabinet), who was quite prepared to offer Churchill a commission as a lieutenant-general. Asquith wanted Churchill to return to London instead, which he did several days later, but not until supervising the entry of a small British force of marines he had organized through the Admiralty.

Belgium did end up surrendering Antwerp and capitulating to the Germans, but the several days' delay that Churchill's visit produced allowed British forces to secure the channel ports. Asquith wrote that "the week at Antwerp was well spent, and had a real effect on the general campaign." But like the "Siege of Sidney Street," Churchill was subjected to fierce criticism for his Antwerp initiative and the comparatively modest British casualties in the operation, criticism he was not able to answer amid the press of urgent war business. But as with other controversial episodes, Churchill did not shrink from saying, "I take the fullest responsibility." After World War II, he wrote, "I certainly bore an exceptional measure of responsibility for the brief and disastrous Norwegian Campaign," even though he could have easily passed the blame to the dithering and temporizing colleagues in the cabinet who slowed up his original design.

At a moment of exasperation over the indecisive and divided counsel of the collective decision making of the war council during World War I, Churchill aptly summarized his principle: "*Someone* has to take the responsibility. I will do so—provided that my decision is the one that rules . . . a man who says, 'I disclaim responsibility for failure,' cannot be the final arbiter of the measures which may be found vital to success." It is not surprising, then, that when faced with criticism in the House of Commons during World War II, Churchill declared: "It follows therefore, when all is said and done, that I am the one whose head should be cut off if we do not win the war."

Simplifying Organizational Structure and Emphasizing Responsibility

This sounds so simple and shopworn as to defy the need of mention, until one asks: Why didn't any of Churchill's colleagues or predecessors make the kind of organizational reforms that mark so many of his administrative posts? When Churchill's organizational practices are examined more closely, it can be seen that the idea of establishing simple organization is not so obvious, especially in a large enterprise.

Like most perceptive observers of human behavior in collective circumstances, Churchill abhorred the tendency of committees and other collective decision-making bodies to be indecisive and irresolute, and especially the tendency of interagency deliberation to weaken still further the effectiveness of collective decision making. In a memorandum at the Admiralty in 1912 Churchill aptly described the problem:

> There is one epicycle of action which is important to avoid, *viz*—recognition of an evil; resolve to deal with it; appointment of a committee to examine it and discover the remedy;

formulation of the remedy; decision to adopt the remedy; consultation with various persons who raise objections; decision to defer to their objections; decision to delay application of the remedy; decision to forget all about the remedy and put up with the evil.

This was a theme he would come to repeat throughout his career. "Everyone claims his margin at every stage," he once complained of interdepartmental deliberations, "and the sum of the margins is usually 'no'." On another occasion he deprecated the Committee on Imperial Defense, which was responsible for general strategic plans but not operations (those were directed by the service chiefs of staff), as representing "the maximum of study and the minimum of action." But the entire structure of British government is based on collective decision making, chiefly conducted through the committee form. How then to produce effective action from collective counsels, especially in wartime when prompt decision making is critical?

Churchill's solution to the problem of collective decision-making dynamics was to couple responsibility with direct power of action. This became the central organizing principle of Churchill's administration. Administrative structure must be clear and precise, with functions divided and responsibility assigned. Above all, overlapping functions were to be avoided. He intensely disliked any committees or organizations that were purely "advisory" in character, or any committees whose chair did not have the full power to make and enforce a decision. "It is easier to give direction than advice," he wrote in his World War II memoirs, "and more agreeable to have the right to act, even in a limited sphere, than the privilege to talk at large." On another occasion Churchill complained that "it is simply darkening counsel to mix up deliberative and advisory committees."

With these hallmarks in mind, Churchill was always able to pare down and streamline his departments, quickly shrinking the number of committees and superfluous administrative structures that had grown like barnacles on the ship of state.

When Churchill became minister of munitions in July 1917, he came to a ministry supervising the productive activities of three million workers at 30,000 firms, with an administrative bureaucracy of 12,000 people divided into 50 different departments, each with a director-general, each reporting to Churchill. "The growth of the Ministry of Munitions had far out-stripped its organization," he wrote later. Churchill was immediately overwhelmed with paperwork and meetings, and the problem of management and coordination of effort was daunting. He disliked having all manner of great and small decisions referred to him alone for disposition. "I set to work at once to divide and distribute this dangerous concentration of power." In place of the 50 existing departments, he set up a Munitions Council of just 10 people, each of whom would be responsible directly to Churchill, and each of whom would now preside over five or six of the previous departments. (The ten departments were: Finance, Design, Steel & Iron, Materials, Explosives, Projectiles, Guns, Engines, Allies, and Labour.) This council met weekly, with Churchill as the chairman. "The relief was instantaneous," Churchill wrote in *The World Crisis*. "I was no longer oppressed by heaps of bulky files. Every one of my ten Councilors was able to give important final decisions in his own sphere. . . . Once the whole organization was in motion it never required change. Instead of struggling through the jungle on foot I rode comfortably on an elephant, whose trunk could pick up a pin or uproot a tree with equal ease, and from whose back a wide scene lay open."

It is important to note here that what Churchill did was *decentralize* the power at the top (his own), through a reorganization that consolidated departments below him. In other words, this was an organizational consolidation that made *delegation* possible. Martin Gilbert wrote that "it was a masterpiece of streamlining."

Churchill also reformed the system of procurement. Under the old scheme, many of the departments would order materials without any coordination with other departments, and without regard to the highest priorities for munitions production. This naturally led to many interdepartmental struggles for scarce materials, and demands on the senior ministers to arbitrate. To solve this problem, Churchill established a centralized council secretariat to manage purchasing and procurement, so that all orders would be in closer harmony with the priorities of the council.

Churchill explained the reason for this reorganization in a ministry memorandum: "It is indispensable that persons near the heads of very large organizations should not be smothered by detail or consume themselves in ordinary day to day business, but that they should have opportunity and freedom to take wide and general views, and to search resolutely and anxiously amid the incidents of business for the dominant truths." Here can be seen the most important reason for having a streamlined organizational structure that emphasizes responsibility: it enables the executives at the top to be more effective. Churchill reiterated this point when he moved to the War Office in 1919, writing to the general in charge of demobilization: "Are you sure you have a big enough machine at the top? . . . The man at the top should not be overloaded: there should be plenty of them, and each should have his sphere, and they should have leisure and a good deal in hand. You cannot possibly do it without wise delegation of powers and a really big machine at the top."

The results of this reorganization were impressive. Despite strikes, labor and material shortages, and the diversion of skilled labor into the armed services, Churchill succeeded in vastly expanding munitions production. In 1918 the army was supplied with more shells than during any other year of the war (42,800 per week—the previous maximum had been 41,000). The production of field guns nearly doubled; the ministry was able to supply about half the guns the arriving American army required. The army deployed twice as many tanks, most of them heavier and faster than earlier models. More than 2,000 tanks were built in 1918; Churchill's plans called for 8,000 in 1919 if the war had continued. Increased aircraft production enabled the number of squadrons to increase from 67 to

200. He established munitions factories in France, so that supplies could be delivered more quickly to the armies in the field.

Churchill's penchant for organizational clarity and simplification continued at his successive posts at the Colonial Office and as chancellor of the exchequer. When Churchill became secretary of state for the colonies in early 1921, he immediately began arguing for a more coherent policy for administering the Empire's holdings in the Middle East. Martin Gilbert paints a brief picture of why such a reorganization was necessary: "Ministerial responsibility [for the Middle East] had been so arranged as to divide up the area between four Departments of State—[Churchill's] own, the India Office, the Colonial Office, and the Foreign Office. Under such a system, it had proved impossible to secure the clear decisions and bold policies which he wanted. The rivalries and conflicting interests of himself [and the other ministers] had paralyzed initiative over a wide area of Government policy." The cabinet finally agreed to Churchill's proposal to form a special Middle East Department within the Colonial Office.

At that time the administration of the Middle East territories was costing Britain £45 million a year, mostly for military protection. "I am determined to save you millions," Churchill told the chancellor of the exchequer. He held a major conference in Cairo to reorganize the territorial boundaries and administrative scheme for the Middle East. The Cairo conference again shows Churchill's organizational mind at work. He divided the work of the conference between two committees, a political committee and a military committee. Churchill had worked out the agendas for the two committees in advance, and he presided over many of the meetings of both committees. The political committee sought to adjust territorial boundaries and to install local leaders to replace colonial administration. (The Feisal family took over in Saudi Arabia as a result of this conference.) The military committee sought to reorganize Britain's military presence in the region to reduce costs. Churchill pressed the committee to probe every item of military expenditure, and complained that the early proposals to reduce costs by £5 million were "quite insufficient." By pressing the committees and demanding more detailed analysis, Churchill succeeded in reducing the annual cost of administering the Middle East from £45 million to £11 million.

Churchill's organizational ideas and experience really came into play when he became prime minister during the war in 1940. Just as in the Ministry of Munitions, Churchill immediately sought to downsize organizational excess. Two weeks after becoming prime minister amid the crisis of the battle of France, Churchill sent a memo to his cabinet secretary: "I am sure there are far too many Committees of one kind or another which Ministers have to attend, and which do not yield a significant result. These should be reduced by suppression or amalgamation." Several months later, Churchill turned his downsizing eye on the number of missions in the United States. The diplomatic overtures to the United States in the fall of 1940, a year before the country entered the war, were at a delicate stage, and Churchill was alarmed at the possible confusion that might result from too many cooks in the kitchen. "Let me have a complete list," he wrote to his cabinet secretary, "of the Missions which we have sent to the United States which are at work there." There turned out to be 11 separate missions in all, some of which, in typical bureaucratic fashion, were intended to be temporary but had taken on an indefinite life, and several more of which overlapped. Churchill ordered an immediate "tidying up." Eventually all the missions involved with procuring military supplies from the United States were consolidated into a single British Supply Council, under the direction of a single chairman.

Churchill's organizational principle of responsibility was especially evident in his restructuring of the war effort. From the outbreak of the war in September 1939 until May 10, 1940 (the day he became prime minister), Churchill served in his World War I post as First Lord of the Admiralty, and as the sole member of Prime Minister Chamberlain's war cabinet with previous experience in the role. The war effort for most of these months suffered from the same tentativeness, confusion, and divided counsel that had plagued the government in World War I. Part of the problem was the lack of strong leadership at the very top—Neville Chamberlain, one high-ranking general later wrote, "presided efficiently over the Cabinet . . . but nothing much happened. . . . He was a fine chairman of a board of directors. He was not the managing director that is necessary in war." But equally part of the problem was cumbersome organization that was not conducive to linear decision making. At nine members, the war cabinet was too large. (This had been a part of the problem with the war council in World War I.) It included the three service ministers (Navy, Army, Air Force) as well as the military chiefs of staff for these three services. This was the first mistake. The service chiefs have executive responsibility for carrying out policy designs that are the product of the political judgment of the elected cabinet members. They are not responsible to Parliament or the voters as are most other ministers. As they are responsible for making *plans* to carry out policy, war cabinet discussions would often be too broad, often extending to the making of operational plans. When the service chiefs objected to certain kinds of plans that were put forward in the cabinet, it tended to redound against policy. At the very least it slowed down the entire process. The problem of coordination among so many different military and civilian departments was too large to be managed at the cabinet level.

The first attempted solution was to form a Military Coordination Committee, chaired by Lord Chatfield, a former First Lord of the Admiralty. This committee was charged with the mission of coordinating the efforts of the military services with the war policy aims set out by the war cabinet. But this committee suffered the defect of being advisory, without actual control of any department, without the power to give orders. The committee was so ineffective that Lord Chatfield resigned, and Chamberlain asked Churchill to take his place. Churchill had no better luck than Chatfield in making the committee an organ for the smooth conduct of the war. Even though the committee met daily, and sometimes twice daily, Churchill chafed that he had "no power to take or enforce decisions." It was, Churchill said, a "fluid, friendly, but unfocused circle." Since the committee had no power of final decision, its frequent internal disagreements were kicked back upstairs to the war cabinet for resolution, defeating the very purpose of the committee. "All had to be explained and re-explained," Churchill wrote in his memoirs, "and by the time this process was completed the whole scene had often changed." Churchill quickly saw that the only means for making the Military Coordination Committee more effective was to have the prime minister himself chair the meetings, which Chamberlain proceeded to do for several weeks. When Chamberlain later considered having Churchill resume the chair of the committee, Churchill demurred, writing to Chamberlain, "I shall not be willing to receive the responsibility back from you without the necessary powers. At present no one has the power. There are six Chiefs of Staff, three Ministers, two C-in-Cs and General Ismay who all have a voice. . . . But no one is now responsible for the creation and direction of military policy except yourself."

When Churchill became prime minister, he decided to sweep away this whole ungainly structure with two bold measures. First, he formed a small war cabinet—only five members, excluding both the three military service ministers and the chiefs of staff. Churchill made an exception to his normal rule that everyone should have some kind of direct departmental responsibility. From now on the war cabinet could deliberate in a more concentrated fashion about broad war policy aims, without the clutter of departmental and service minutiae. "The days of mere 'coordination' were out for good," one senior military figure wrote later. "We were now going to get direction, leadership, action—with a snap in it!"

But it was Churchill's second act that was more significant: he named himself as minister of defense, thereby placing himself in the direct line of authority for the creation of war plans and their execution. (Churchill had advocated merging the three fighting services under a single minister of defense as far back as 1919, as a way of improving wartime coordination of effort and reducing interservice rivalry.) This arrangement put Churchill in direct contact with the service chiefs of staff, whose meetings he would sometimes chair, though usually, Churchill wrote, "It is my practice to leave the Chiefs of Staff alone to do their own work, subject to my general supervision, suggestion, and guidance." Most important, Churchill did not create a new Ministry of Defense with the usual administrative bureaucracy; indeed, although he secured the king's permission to become minister of defense, he did not seek an act of Parliament to create either the position or a new ministry to support it. But it was the lack of formal organization that was the key to its effectiveness.

Martin Gilbert describes the nature and importance of this arrangement in his biography of Churchill:

> It was in his combined capacity as Prime Minister and Minister of Defense that he was able to supervise the war effort both as the ultimate authority, and as specific overlord of defense policy. Yet his control of defense was not through a great department of State with its myriad officials, its national and local offices, its agents and its emissaries. Instead, it was a single office headed by Ismay, and with a small staff. "I clearly remember," Ismay wrote to Churchill six years later, "that one of the first things that you said to me after you assumed the office of Minister of Defense, was 'we must be very careful not to define our powers too precisely.'"

"I was soon able to give an integral direction to almost every aspect of the war," Churchill wrote.

Although the Military Coordination Committee passed from the scene because of this reformed scheme, Churchill was not able to abolish the Joint Planning Staff, which was a creation of the three military services and was intended to coordinate the plans of the three military services. The Joint Planning Staff essentially just reviewed the plans agreed upon by the chiefs of staff, usually raising questions and concerns that cast doubt on such plans. Again, this was more of an advisory than an executive body, and as such Churchill regarded it as "the dead weight of inertia and delay," and referred to it another time as "the whole machinery of negation." The Joint Planning Staff was an official instrument of the military, so Churchill lacked the direct authority to abolish it outright; he sought to bring it under his control by having it work directly under himself in his capacity as minister of defense.

Just as he had with the Ministry of Munitions in World War I, Churchill divided up the war effort in his *de facto* Ministry of Defense into clearly divided subcommittees. In this case, the two principal subcommittees were the Supply Committee and the Operations Committee. Each committee comprised the various ministers whose functions were relevant. Churchill chaired both committees.

Maintaining Flexibility

An important corollary to Churchill's administrative principles was *flexibility*. He was not bound by any of the administrative arrangements he set in motion, and would occasionally violate the strict simplicity of his committee structure either by breaking off one function into its own full-fledged ministry, or more often by the use of an ad hoc committee for a specific problem. For example, even though questions of supply were the domain of the Supply Committee, which included the air minister, Churchill saw fit to create a separate Ministry of Aircraft, which he assigned to his longtime friend Lord Beaverbrook to oversee. Because aircraft production loomed more important than any other supply question in the early days of the war, when air superiority would mean the life or death of the nation in the Battle of Britain in a few months' time, the creation of a separate ministry was justified. This arrangement produced immediate results. On another occasion, Churchill created a new Ministry of Transport, to unify shipping and surface transportation under a single minister who could then coordinate land and sea transportation better than separate ministers could.

The ad hoc committee was used more frequently. Churchill set in motion 75 ad hoc committees during his first year as prime minister. When losses due to submarine attacks became critical in late 1940, Churchill expanded the war cabinet into the "Battle of the Atlantic Committee" to concentrate on this single problem.

The key to the smooth, effective functioning of his administrative apparatus was a competent personal office of secretaries and assistants who served as the conduit for information and directives. Way back in 1917, when Churchill reorganized the Ministry of Munitions, he had observed:

> Another indispensable feature of office organization lies in the development of a trained and efficient Secretariat. The direction and distribution of the flow of official papers among all departments, and the means taken to concert the action of the various departments and authorities concerned in each class of business, the recording of action and the circulation of information of all kinds, constitute a sphere second only in importance to decisions on policy and merits.

Finally, Churchill was fond of the occasional shakeup, seeing that even a clear and responsible organizational scheme could become ineffective with the passage of time and the accretion of detail that necessarily occurs in any organizational enterprise. Sometimes it is better simply to replace the old organization and its managers with a new organization with fresh blood at the top. In late 1941, for example, Churchill set up a new Production Executive to replace the existing Production Council, which had grown into a "large, amorphous, and ineffective body" (as one of Churchill's aides put it) under its present chairman, Arthur Greenwood. This kind of reorganization cuts out the existing bureaucracy and stifling procedure at a single stroke. In 1942, Churchill changed the command structure of Middle East forces while on a visit, commenting that "I must emphasize the need of a new start and vehement action to animate the whole of this vast but baffled and somewhat unhinged organization."

CHURCHILL'S ADMINISTRATIVE LESSONS

• *Take responsibility.*
Churchill's maxim: "Someone has to take responsibility. I will."

• *In the absence of responsible leadership, collective decision-making bodies will temporize.*
Churchill's maxim: "Everyone claims his margin at every stage, and the sum of the margins is usually 'no'."

• *Simplify through delegation that concentrates your effective power.*
Churchill's maxim: "It is indispensable that persons near the heads of very large organizations should not be smothered by detail or consume themselves in ordinary day to day business, but that they should have opportunity and freedom to take wide and general views, and to search resolutely and anxiously amid the incidents of business for the dominant truths."

• *The corollary: Maintain flexibility and use ad hoc structures for particular problems.*

CHAPTER 5

CHURCHILL
ON PERSONNEL

Managing People and Managing Yourself

———————◆◆◆———————

You cannot build a Staff as you build a house, from the bottom up-
wards, and then when it is all finished put the Chief of Staff on top of
it like the chimney.

— WINSTON S. CHURCHILL, 1912

F INDING THE RIGHT people to fill key positions is equal in importance to having the right organizational structure. "By and large," Peter Drucker has written, "executives make poor promotion and staffing decisions. By all accounts, their batting average is no better than .333: at most one-third of such decisions turn out right; one-third are minimally effective; and one-third are outright failures."

The refinements of personnel questions are too often neglected by managers who look only at the qualifications and experience on a résumé, and do not give sufficient thought to matching the character of the individual with the character of the job and the need of the moment. Personnel selection and management comprises three essential factors: finding the right people, getting them to work together toward your goals, and making sure you listen to what they have to say.

Churchill understood that key personnel not only execute policy but also serve as the prime conduit for information that the person at the top needs to follow up on old decisions as well as make new decisions. Second, to adapt the old saying about doctors ("Physician: heal thyself"), managers must be able to manage themselves before they can manage others. Rare is the successful leader or executive with a chaotic mind or chaotic habits. How Churchill managed himself goes hand-in-hand with how he managed people. Churchill's approach once again supplies a unique perspective to this fundamental executive task.

Churchill's Principles and Practices for Selecting People

Churchill acted according to three basic principles when it came to picking personnel. First, ignore seniority, and pick the person you think is best suited for the job. Second, have your main plans in mind *before* you pick your executives, so that they are serving *your* designs and not their own. Third, start at the top, rather than at the bottom. Following these principles allowed Churchill to range more widely over the whole scene, secure that his particular designs would be faithfully executed by capable lieutenants.

Churchill has often been criticized for having poor judgment about people, or for having played favorites with friends and desiring to be surrounded by yes-men and sycophants. These criticisms are largely unfounded or exaggerated. "While Churchill could undervalue a good but silent man," military historian Maxwell Schoenfled has written, "he usually picked able men to serve him. There were no empty-headed sycophants assembled for the weekends at Chequers." And one of his senior military commanders during World War II wrote: "He hated yes-men—he had no use for them. What he wanted was people who would stand up to him."

To be sure, Churchill favored large personalities, and was not averse to selecting people for important posts who had been subject to severe criticism and opposition in the past—in other words, people who were much like himself. He understood that such people often possessed not only a strong character, but an independence of judgment and action that was the one thing most needful in time of war. Such people will eventually come to command the respect of their peers. Churchill had begun to absorb this lesson while still a young man. In *The River War*, written when he was just

25, Churchill observes this independence of character in the person of Charles Gordon, the famous British commander killed by the Sudanese in Khartoum. "Perhaps it is because he is careless of the sympathy of men," Churchill wrote, "that Charles Gordon so readily wins it."

A few weeks after he became prime minister, Churchill wrote in a memorandum to Foreign Secretary Anthony Eden:

> There is a great opportunity now for picking leaders, not only among those who have had the opportunity of meeting the enemy, but also in those who have prepared themselves to do so. *Men of force and intelligence and personality,* who would make their way to leading positions in civil life, should be given their chance as soon as they have acquired the minim of training. *We want live wires, and not conventional types.* (Emphasis added.)

Six months later Churchill reiterated this theme, writing to General Sir John Dill, "We cannot afford to confine Army appointments to persons who have excited no hostile comment in their careers. . . . This is a time to try men of force and vision and not to be exclusively confined to those who are judged thoroughly safe by conventional standards." He reiterated this theme in 1943, writing to the chiefs of staff that "no mere question of seniority must obstruct the advance of real personalities to their proper stations in war." He defended a young officer he favored against criticism by saying, "Such prejudices attach frequently to persons of strong personality and original views."

Churchill had long and sometimes painful experience in selecting unconventional and controversial people for top posts, so when he offered this audacious counsel in World War II he did so with the full weight of authority that such experience confers. When he became First Lord of the Admiralty in 1911, one of his first acts was to appoint Rear-Admiral John Beatty to be his private secretary at the Admiralty. Beatty had a controversial past. Although recognized as an officer of courage and experience, he had declined an appointment to command the Atlantic Fleet a few years before—a step usually fatal to a naval career in those days. Because of this and other factors, Churchill had been "advised about him at the Admiralty in a decisively adverse sense."

> But my first meeting with the Admiral induced me immediately
> to disregard this unfortunate advice. . . . It became increasingly
> clear to me that he viewed questions of naval strategy and tactics in a different light than the average officer: he approached
> them, as it seemed to me, much more as a soldier would. . . .
> He thought of war problems in their unity by land, sea, and air.

Churchill was shortly to appoint Beatty to a senior fleet command, and several years later recommended him to be First Sea Lord.

Churchill's most controversial appointment was Lord John Fisher, whom Churchill selected to be First Sea Lord, the number two job at the Admiralty after Churchill himself, in 1914. Lord Fisher had been First Sea Lord once before, from 1904 to 1910, and his tenure in that post had been highly controversial. He had successfully pushed for the development of the submarine, larger battleships with larger guns and bigger engines, and the scrapping of obsolete ships, among other things. This was during the period when the Germans were attempting to build a navy to rival Britain's. The navy had resisted many of his changes and innovations. "Harsh, capricious, vindictive, gnawed by hatreds arising often from spite," Churchill wrote of Fisher many years later in *Great Contemporaries*, "working secretly or violently as occasion might suggest by methods which the typical English gentleman and public-school boy are taught to dislike and avoid, Fisher was always regarded as the 'dark angel' of the Naval service. . . . 'Ruthless, relentless, and remorseless' were the epithets he sought always to associate with himself." In *The World Crisis*, Churchill concluded that "There is no doubt that Fisher was right in nine-tenths of what he fought for.

His great reforms sustained the power of the Royal Navy at the most critical period in its history. He gave the Navy the kind of shock which the British Army received at the time of the South African War. . . . The originality of his mind and the spontaneity of his nature freed him from conventionalities of all kinds."

"Favoritism is the secret of efficiency," Fisher had once written. Churchill heartily concurred: "What he meant by 'favoritism' was selection without regard to seniority by a discerning genius in the interests of the public." Fisher was exactly the kind of unconventional, large personality Churchill sought to help him with his plans to modernize the fleet and install a naval war staff. Churchill first turned to Fisher in an advisory capacity in 1912, when the program to convert the fleet from coal to oil began. "This liquid fuel problem has got to be solved," Churchill wrote in his letter inviting Fisher to take up the task, "and the natural, inherent, unavoidable difficulties are such that they require the drive and enthusiasm of a big man. I want you for this, viz, to crack the nut. No one else can do it so well. Perhaps no one else can do it at all. I will put you in a position where you can crack the nut, if indeed it is crackable."

When war broke out in 1914 and the current First Sea Lord, Prince Louis of Battenburg, resigned because of his family tie to the German Emperor, Churchill immediately sought to bring back Fisher as First Sea Lord. The King and many others objected to this controversial personality, but Churchill persevered (partly by threatening resignation if he didn't get his way) and the Fisher appointment was made. It had exactly the effect Churchill hoped. Martin Gilbert wrote: "At the Admiralty Fisher served as the spark to ignite a hundred trains of powder." In *The World Crisis*, Churchill commented on the working relationship these two dominating personalities forged:

> We made the agreement between ourselves that neither of us should take any important action without consulting the other, unless previous accord had been reached. To this agreement we

both scrupulously adhered. We had thus formed, for the first time, an overwhelmingly strong control and central authority over the whole course of the naval war, and were in a position to make our will prevail throughout the fleets and all branches of the naval administration, as well as to hold our own against all outside interference.

But Fisher was 75 years old at the time, and the strain of the war took its toll on his volatile personality. He threatened resignation more than 10 times over the next nine months, and he eventually played a central role in Churchill's downfall from the Admiralty over the Dardanelles fiasco. Churchill was convinced ever after that Fisher had suffered a nervous breakdown, and even though Fisher had dealt Churchill a serious blow, Churchill was not deterred from his appreciation of Fisher's abilities, or his own penchant for picking large and controversial personalities for important posts. Years later, after Fisher's death, Churchill reflected in *Great Contemporaries*:

> My bringing Fisher back to the Admiralty in 1914 was one of the most hazardous steps I have ever had to take in my official duty. Certainly, so far as I was concerned, it was the most disastrous. Yet looking back to those tragic years I cannot feel that if I had to repeat the decision with the knowledge I had at that time, I should act differently. Fisher brought to the Admiralty an immense wave of enthusiasm for the construction of warships. His genius was mainly that of a constructor, organizer and energizer.

In World War II Churchill once again overrode the objections of the King and others to appoint Lord Max Beaverbrook to direct aircraft production. Beaverbrook was a Canadian who had made a fortune in Canada many years before by methods that were widely rumored to have been ruthless or unscrupulous, and though he had been a close friend of Churchill's for many years, his reputation was decidedly mixed. Aircraft production doubled over the next few months under Beaverbrook's aggressive prodding, justifying Churchill's estimate that Beaverbrook "had genius, and also brutal ruthlessness."

Churchill believed that in selecting personnel you should start at the top. At the outset of his reorganization of the naval staff in 1912, Churchill wrote to Prime Minister Asquith: "I must have the principal men in their places. You cannot build a Staff as you build a house, from the bottom upwards, and then when it is all finished put the Chief of Staff on top of it like the chimney. One has to go the other way round and organize a good group of men at the top and let them work out the details in accordance with principles which have been clearly prescribed."

But it was equally important, Churchill thought, that key strategic decisions should be made before selecting the top people. In an instructive memorandum to Prime Minister David Lloyd-George that Churchill wrote in 1919 after he had moved to the War Office, he advocated the case for appointing Lord Beatty as First Sea Lord—but not until after new policy had been decided:

> At any rate it seems to me that sooner or later Beatty will have to replace Wemyss [as First Sea Lord], and in a reasonable time. I think this would be the right thing to do. On the other hand you must remember that once Beatty is enthroned he will be in a position to champion the particularist interest of the Admiralty to an extent it would be quite impossible for Wemyss to do. It is therefore extremely important that no change should take place at the present time, that the main finance of the three Services should be discussed and adjusted, and that any newcomer should be invited to come in on the basis that he accepts in principle the decisions arrived at.

An important corollary to this point is the necessity of providing clear instruction to subordinate executives. "It is essential," Churchill wrote in a memorandum at about this same time, "that you should beforehand give the decisions which will allow your lieutenants to act effectively."

Like any leader, Churchill had to dismiss people from time to time. William Ewart Gladstone, a long-running prime minister during the late 19th century (Churchill's father, Lord Randolph, had battled against Gladstone) had said that the first essential for a prime minister is to be "a good butcher." Asquith had reminded Churchill of this remark when he offered Churchill his first cabinet post in 1908. Despite this necessity, Churchill never relished the role of butcher. "He pretended to a ruthlessness which was entirely foreign to his nature," Colville wrote, while John Martin (another of Churchill's personal secretaries) wrote of his "agony of reluctance before dismissing a loyal minister when Cabinet changes were necessary." General Ironside, whom Churchill dismissed as commander-in-chief of home forces in 1940, wrote that "I don't suppose that Winston liked doing it, for he is always loyal to his friends."

The loyalty Ironside speaks of here was an attribute that Churchill extended to all who served him, not just his friends. People who had been selected for military command or important office could expect Churchill's unwavering support in return for the high responsibility he expected them to exercise. "Backing people up" was a cardinal principle. If someone was in difficulty, Churchill thought it was essential not to waver or equivocate: "You must either wallop a man or vindicate him," Churchill said. Churchill's support was especially stout if appointees faced difficult circumstances. To General Wavell, commander of British forces in the Middle East, Churchill wrote that he was prepared to "take the rough with the smooth," and that Wavell should "be quite sure that we will back you up in adversity even better than in good fortune." Sir Leslie Rowan, another of his many private secretaries, wrote that "Churchill never let down his staff," while another of his secretaries wrote that, as a member of his personal staff, "You were treated as part of the family, on the basis of complete trust."

Churchill sought to cement this intimate, trustworthy atmosphere with social occasions outside the office. Such social contact, he understood, would contribute to the general esprit de corps of the entire leadership. As minister of munitions, Churchill had established a luncheon club "for the 60 or 70 officers of the Ministry. This would enable them to meet in twos and threes in *quiet* and agreeable surroundings daily. Everyone will get to know the other. 'Shop' could be talked under good auspices." When he returned to the Admiralty in 1939, Churchill instituted a regular Tuesday night dinner party, to which he would have 14 guests each week drawn from various government ministries and military services.

It is often said, based on anecdotes about Churchill's brief interviews with people he subsequently selected for appointment, that Churchill judged people quickly, perhaps too quickly. But he employed a simple method for determining whether people had the one quality he valued above all others: candor and direct plain-spokenness. In his account of his introductory interview with Churchill in 1941, Sir Leslie Rowan sheds considerable light on this aspect of Churchill:

> As he spoke he wheeled round me so as to get a good view of my face with the light at his back and not in his eyes. He liked to see the faces of those he had to deal with, and often made judgments on what he saw. He asked me about my career, or rather told me, as John Martin had, as usual, briefed him well. Then came the questions, "And what do you now do at the Treasury?"—he knew quite well, of course. I started to reply, "I deal with the supply side of Naval expenditure," and, before I could go on, he said, "Trying to cut it down, no doubt?" I replied, "Yes, sir, I do my best." After a slight pause, "Well, I suppose someone has to do it; thank you so much for coming to see me," and he went on his way to lunch. Next day I heard that I had been appointed.

Looking back, I am sure this was a test. He hated above most things what he called "the official grimace." Provided you told the truth and had some real conviction about and basis for your views, you had a fair hearing, and he was open to argument. If I had fluffed this answer, and made some polite but insincere remarks designed to please, I am convinced that I should not have been appointed.

Churchill also dismissed several candidates after an equally abrupt examination, according to John Martin, one of his many private secretaries. (Martin had been appointed after a similarly brief interview.)

Churchill, like any executive with a long tenure, made his share of mistakes and misjudgments about people. Sometimes his appointees didn't get along with each other. Sometimes they suffered burnout. On the whole, however, Churchill was well-served by his central guidelines about selecting personnel.

Keep Fully Informed, Firsthand

It is commonplace today to speak of "information overload," but few executives have had to cope with as many dimensions of information flow as Churchill did in World War II. As with so many aspects of Churchill's executive leadership, he brought several levels of refinement to a task that all executives and leaders face. Seeking information for Churchill served at least three functions: as a way of concentrating the minds of his subordinates on the most important things at hand, as a way of preparing for deliberations, and as a way of cutting through bureaucracy. For Churchill, his key personnel served as his primary information feedback loop.

Churchill always liked to get information direct and unfiltered. "He did not like information served up to him second-hand," Sir Ian Jacob wrote. He not only wished to see copies of all operational telegrams sent from the chiefs of staff to commanders in the field, but he also insisted on seeing the raw transcripts of decrypted messages intercepted by British intelligence, rather than have paraphrased or edited reports about what the intercepts contained. Few phrases are more common in Churchill's vast correspondence than "Let me have a report as to what is happening." "From each of his minutes," Martin Gilbert wrote, "Churchill expected to learn what was happening over the full range of his responsibilities, and to probe every area of potential war policy and action." Churchill followed through on these requests, emphasizing their importance to his task. He would remind colleagues and subordinates if they failed to make their reports, or if they were deficient in some way. To his close friend Professor Frederick Lindemann, Churchill sent a minute saying, "You are not presenting me as I should like every few days, or every week, with a short clear statement of the falling off or improvement in munitions production. I am not able to form a clear view unless you do this."

Many of his inquiries to government officials were prompted by items he had seen in the newspapers, of which Churchill was a voracious reader. "With breakfast," John Peck wrote, "he would always examine the daily newspapers, at least nine in number. He always did this himself and never relied on any press reader or system of clipping or marking."

Above all, Churchill understood the power and usefulness of information as a means of cutting through bureaucratic inertia and obfuscation. Churchill, according to one of his senior military advisers, had an "instinctive distrust of large organizations, whether civil or military. He was suspicious of what would happen to any question when it passed on the line into the depth of some great Department." It is in the nature of any large organization, whether a public bureaucracy or a corporate bureaucracy, to produce information and evidence that are most favorable to its own point of view. Churchill sought to conquer this problem by forming his own statistical office that would gather information and statistics on all aspects of the war effort, and report directly to him. This was by now an old practice for Churchill. He was one of the first modern political leaders to recognize the value of statistics and quantitative analysis. He had appointed a statistical adviser when he was minister of munitions in 1917, and at the Admiralty he used a system of 23 charts—many of them updated daily—as the means of keeping track of all vital aspects of naval activity. Churchill appointed his close friend Professor Lindemann, who had been advising him on scientific matters for some years, to head his statistical office in World War II. (Lindemann was a professor of physics at Oxford University.) This statistical office consisted of about 20 people, comprising economists, at least one scientist, civil servants, and the usual retinue of clerk-typists to produce the written reports.

With his statistical unit, one of his private secretaries observed, Churchill was able to send to his ministers "a stream of written requests for monthly, fortnightly, weekly, or even daily returns on production, technical developments, manpower, training, tank and aircraft strength, which he would then scrutinize with care." This independent source of information and review allowed Churchill to keep abreast of a multitude of activities, and to make specific requests for further information or action. Martin Gilbert notes that "Churchill did not regard statistics as things to be manipulated in order to advance a particular policy." In one of his minutes to Lindemann he makes clear that he saw statistics as a tool for finding out what is taking place: "Do not think of making a case for a particular point of view," Churchill wrote, "Let us just have the cold-blooded facts."

Because of these practices, Churchill was typically the best-informed person in the cabinet, and could not be snowed by jargon-speaking civil servants. Sir Ian Jacob noted that "He came well prepared to all the [war cabinet] meetings. The other Ministers may not have read the telegrams—their senior officials had read them of course, and briefed them on that basis—but Churchill had read them himself."

Stay Disciplined about Your Priorities

Churchill understood that the task of managing a large number of people in important jobs depended upon his ability to manage himself. By no other means would it be possible to give clear direction and to keep control over the vast war machinery. "In any sphere of action there can be no comparison between the positions of number one and numbers two, three, or four," Churchill wrote after the war. "The duties and problems of all persons other than number one are quite different and in many ways more difficult."

Self-management at the top requires sensible priorities. Setting priorities is one thing. As an intellectual exercise, just about anyone can set priorities. Sticking to them requires consistent discipline.

This would seem to be especially a problem for Churchill, whose restless, wide-ranging mind was so frequently commented upon by friend and critic alike. His high energy level and enthusiasm for all aspects of what was going on would seem to make it difficult to discern priorities, let alone stick to them. His attention to detail, which to his critics often bordered on meddling, was another aspect of his management style that could easily be thought to dilute focus. "Churchill was always a man capable of operating on many fronts simultaneously," Randolph Churchill wrote in his biography of his father. "He is here, there, and everywhere," a colleague at the Admiralty noted of Churchill in 1912.

Through this whirlwind, however, Churchill was remarkably disciplined. Despite his wide-ranging attention and interests, he always kept in mind what was centrally important to the moment. He was always able to focus his full concentration on the immediate task at hand, and he sent clear signals to his subordinates when an inquiry or directive was of special importance. "When his mind was occupied with any particular problem," Sir Ian Jacob wrote, "it was relentlessly focused upon it and would not be turned aside." Ultimately this served as the cornerstone of his time-management system.

"His general method of work," wrote Lord Normanbrook, a member of his cabinet secretariat during World War II, "was to concentrate his personal attention on the two or three things that mattered most at any given moment, and to give to each of these all the time and attention that it merited. He had a remarkable intuitive capacity for picking out the questions on which he could most usefully concentrate his effort."

In World War II the dominant long-term factor that claimed top priority was the question of material and supply. Way back in 1898 Churchill had written in *The River War* that "even the military student, in his zeal to master the fascinating combinations of the actual conflict, often forgets the far more intricate complications of supply." Churchill would not forget this vital factor. Colville noted in his diary in June 1940 that Churchill "is also taking the question of supply very seriously and has meetings almost every morning now."

Churchill's other notable innovation of the time was his use of the red "Action This Day" tabs he would attach to minutes and memoranda that demanded immediate attention. (These could be considered an early form of the Post-It note.) Churchill instituted these labels in February 1940 while he was at the Admiralty, after being upset and frustrated at the lack of follow-through on several important supply questions. He used a few variations of these tabs—besides "Action This Day," he also used yellow tabs reading "Report in Three Days" and "Report Progress in One Week."

Stick to a Method

Churchill's peripatetic mind, his relentless prodding and probing, and his endless energy have misled many into supposing that he was undisciplined or unfocused. But in fact he was highly methodical. He had to be methodical if for no other reason than to get through the huge amount of paperwork that he generated and demanded. "His concentration was made possible by the way in which he conducted his business," Sir Ian Jacob wrote.

Much has been made of Churchill's eccentricities: the omnipresent cigars, the regular afternoon naps, the habit of dictating in bed or in the bathtub (on either of his two daily baths), the way he kept his secretaries and assistants up until the small hours of the night. This seemingly odd routine was the key to his extraordinary productivity. One of his literary assistants, Bill Deakin, described Churchill as "absolutely totally organized, almost like a clock. . . . His routine was absolutely dictatorial. He set himself a ruthless timetable every day and would get very agitated and cross if it was broken." The regular afternoon nap, which he kept up even on most of his travels, was a major key to his extraordinary productivity. By taking a 60- to 90-minute nap every day, followed by a second hot bath after he awoke, Churchill could press a day and a half's work into one. This odd routine required "an elaborate arrangement of shifts" among his secretaries and assistants.

Churchill was like an engineer in the sequential, orderly way he approached his workday, and the tasks before him. "Design" and "plan" were two of his favorite nouns. "Proceeding by design through crisis to decision" is a typical Churchill formula. "'Step by Step' is a valuable precept," he wrote to Fisher in 1912—a maxim that he would restate in various forms throughout his career.

The organization of Churchill's paperwork flow displays the kind of many-layered scheme he would employ. He had his staff divide his incoming paperwork into eleven categories:

- Top of the box (most important or urgent matters)
- Foreign Office telegrams
- Service telegrams
- Periodical returns (regular reports he had requested)

- Parliamentary questions
- For signature
- To see
- General Ismay (reports from chief of staff)
- Answers other (other people besides Ismay)
- Ecclesiastical
- R Week-end (low priority items to get to on the weekend)

Churchill occasionally fell behind on his paperwork, and sometimes deigned to go through papers of lower priority, but on the whole he stuck faithfully to this system throughout the war, and would frequently get all the way through to "the bottom of the box."

Organizational structure and discipline alone are not sufficient to make for successful administration. What made Churchill's administrative schemes work was his decision-making ability, his communication ability, and a variety of other character traits that complete the arsenal of virtues required for effective leadership. The next three chapters take these up in turn.

CHURCHILL'S GUIDELINES

- *On selecting and managing personnel:*
Start at the top.
Seek large personalities and unconventional types; ignore seniority.
Have your plans in place *before* making the selection.
Establish trust.
Give clear direction.
Back up your people through thick and thin.

- *Provide clear direction.*
Churchill's maxim: "It is essential that you should beforehand give the decisions which will allow your lieutenants to act effectively."

• *Keep fully informed; get your information direct.*

• *Stick to priorities.*

Churchill's practice: Work on the two or three most important things at the moment.

• *Have a consistent method and discipline.*

Churchill's maxims: "'Step by Step' is a valuable precept." "Seek to proceed by design through crisis to decision."

CHAPTER 6

THE POWER OF DECISION

Churchill's Thought Process

———————◆◆◆———————

If we look back on our past life we shall see that one of its most usual experiences is that we have been helped by our mistakes and injured by our most sagacious decisions.

—WINSTON S. CHURCHILL, 1932

It is always wise to look ahead, but difficult to look farther than you can see.

—WINSTON S. CHURCHILL, 1952

W AR DECISIONS OFFER a close parallel in form to entrepreneurial decisions. Both the war leader and the entrepreneur or CEO need to be able to judge *risk* and *chance*. Information is usually limited or insufficient to provide certainty as to the outcome of a venture. One can't be sure how the enemy (the competition) will respond. Hence almost all decisions must be made in the shadow of uncertainty. Most people shrink from risk and are unable to reach firm decisions because they are paralyzed by uncertainty. Churchill remarked that it is never possible to guarantee success; it is only possible to deserve it. One deserves success only by reaching and implementing clear and consistent decisions, and factoring in the element of chance by some method. Chapter 1 commented on Churchill's decisiveness and the historical imagination that informed his decisions, especially his war decisions. This chapter takes a closer look at Churchill's thought process and at the do's and don'ts derived from his deliberations about how decisions should be reached.

Churchill held that there were three positive hallmarks (do's) of effective thinking, and three common errors (don'ts) to be avoided. The three hallmarks: always keep the central or most important aspect of the current problem in mind, know how to balance the chances on both sides of a decision and keep these factors in proportion, and remain open to changing your mind in the presence of new facts.

The three common errors: trying to look too far ahead, trying for excessive perfection, and making decisions for decision's sake that would better be postponed or not made at all. These errors of decision making are all matters of degree—one must look ahead, try to make the best decision possible, and reach essential decisions briskly; but it is as dangerous to go too far in any of the three areas as to do too little with them. Contrary to the oft-conveyed impression that Churchill was a stubborn bully perpetually demanding his own way in meetings, Churchill's thoughts and decisions were aided always by extensive deliberation and consultation with his aides and colleagues. It was typical of Churchill to go around the table and ask all the participants in a meeting for their independent views on the issue at hand. Moreover, although Churchill often argued vehemently with his military chiefs of staff during World War II, he never overruled their opinions, and deferred to their counsel on dozens of occasions where he had originally sought a different course.

HALLMARKS OF EFFECTIVE THOUGHT

Take the Broad View; Concentrate on the Central Point

Frederick the Great said that "sensible men concentrate on the essential," and Churchill took this maxim to heart to a higher degree than any modern statesman. Churchill was always focused on the "broad view" or the "center point of any thought," as he put it. Throughout both World War I and World War II, Churchill would periodically produce long memoranda summarizing the general scene of the war at the present moment, pointing out what had changed since previous decisions had been made, and where new opportunities and vulnerabilities were. He used these reviews to brief the House of Commons on the state of the war, and he also relied on this method as a way of preparing for his summit meetings with President Roosevelt and Marshall Stalin. "It is perhaps a good thing," he wrote on one of his trans-Atlantic sailings to Washington D.C. during the war, "to stand away from the canvas from time to time and take a full view of the picture."

Just as an entrepreneur or CEO must have a large view of the essential ingredients of a successful business strategy (that is, sufficient working capital, or an extensive sales and marketing apparatus, or a clear identification of the core business), Churchill always zoomed in on the key factor or factors required for victory. The important point to grasp, however, is that it is only when one has a broad view or clear understanding of the central aspects of the problem at hand that it becomes possible for the necessary details to fall into place. Few phrases are more common in Churchill's memoranda and speeches than "All these questions can be settled harmoniously if they are related to some central design." In example after example, it is possible to see how Churchill's general view, his penchant for focusing on a deliberate design, guided all of his particular decisions and actions.

In *The River War*, his account of Lord Kitchener's conquest of the Sudan in 1898 (where Churchill served as a junior officer and war correspondent), Churchill could see that the dominant factor was *supply*, which had to be built up and extended patiently into the African interior over a two-year period. "In a tale of war," Churchill wrote, "the reader's mind is filled with the fighting. . . . The long trailing line of communications is unnoticed. . . . Victory is the beautiful, bright-colored flower. Transport is the stem without which it could never have blossomed. Yet even the military student, in his zeal to master the fascinating combinations of the actual conflict, often forgets the far more intricate complications of supply." In the case of the Sudan campaign, providing the supply for a large mobile army required the construction of a railway across the desert, and a constant stream of riverboats bearing supplies up the Nile. It was through his observations of the thoroughness of these preparations that Churchill acquired his inclination to look into countless supply and logistical details in World War II.

In his chapter in the role of supply and the construction of the desert railway in *The River War*, the managerial Churchill shines through:

> The questions to be decided were numerous and involved. How much carrying capacity was required? How much rolling stock? How many engines? What spare parts? How much oil? How many lathes? How many cutters? How many punching and shearing machines? What arrangement of signals would be necessary? How many lamps? How many points? How many trolleys? What amount of coal should be ordered? How much water would be wanted? How should it be carried? To what extent would its carriage affect the hauling power and influence all previous calculations? How much railway plant was needed? How many miles of rail? How many thousand sleepers? Where could they be procured at such short notice? How many fish-plates were necessary? What tools would be required? What appliances? What machinery? How much skilled labor was wanted? How much of the class of labor available? How were the workmen to be fed and watered? How much food would they want? How many trains a day must be run to feed them and their escort? How many must be run to carry plant? How did these requirements affect the estimate for rolling stock? The answers to all these questions, and to many others with which I will not inflict the reader, were set forth by Lieutenant Girouard [the officer in charge of the project] in a ponderous volume several inches thick; and such was the comprehensive accuracy of the estimate that the working parties were never delayed by the want of a piece of brass wire.

It was because of these patient and painstaking preparations, Churchill wrote, that the Sudanese were "conquered on the railway." (It is also worth noting that the entire campaign was conducted within the budget appropriated for it by the British government.)

For several years before the outbreak of World War I, Churchill had been warning that any new European war would be of an entirely different character from previous wars, on account of modern weapons and the rapidly advancing industrial economies of nations that would tend to involve much larger portions of their populations either as production workers or as soldiers. Churchill had in fact anticipated what subsequently became known as "total war." Whereas many previous wars were often decided in single decisive episodes on the battlefield, Churchill understood that 20th-century war would be decided as much in the factories at home as on the battlefield itself. "The old wars were decided by their episodes rather than by their tendencies," Churchill told the House of Commons in 1915. "In this War the tendencies are far more important than the episodes." Hence when Churchill became minister of munitions in 1917, he circulated a memorandum to the entire ministry pointing out the central importance of the raw material for all modern weapons: steel.

"This is a Steel War," Churchill wrote. "The foundation upon which all our chances of Victory stand is Steel. . . . Steel is not only our principal means of war, but it is our best chance of saving the lives of our soldiers. This is a war of machinery; and generalship consists in using machinery instead of flesh and blood to achieve the purposes of strategy and tactics." In an effort to procure the maximum amount of steel possible, Churchill circulated another memo enumerating every possible source of iron that might be scavenged, including the iron railings in London parks. "I should suppose there were 20,000 tons of iron in the Hyde Park railings alone, while the weight of metal in the area railings of the London streets must be enormous."

In the course of World War II, it is possible to discern the shifts of the central features of the war as the war situation gradually changed. In the early days of Churchill's premiership in 1940, he placed emphasis on aircraft production (especially fighters), understanding that the coming air battle would determine whether Britain would survive at all to carry on the war. With the successful outcome of the Battle of Britain in the fall of 1940, Churchill turned his main attention to the submarine threat to British shipping. German U-boats were exacting a huge toll on shipping of vital war material from America, and if the U-boat menace could not be stopped Britain's ability to carry on the war would be in serious doubt. Churchill decided to elevate the matter to the highest priority, first by publicly declaring "The Battle of the Atlantic," and then by forming a special "Battle of the Atlantic Committee" to meet regularly to consider and orchestrate countermeasures.

During the war's darkest hours in 1940, Churchill told the Soviet ambassador that his plan was "to survive the next six weeks," but even at that adverse moment Churchill was looking ahead and laying plans for eventual victory. He queried the responsible ministers about long-range plans for the production of sufficient numbers of landing craft, without which no invasion of Europe would be possible. It was also early in the war that Churchill pushed the idea for concrete harbors—later to be code named *Mulberries*—that could be towed across the English Channel and sunk in shallow waters to create artificial harbors for supply ships.

As Britain first survived the blitz in the fall of 1940 and then gained the upper hand over German U-boats as America entered the war in 1941, Churchill kept revising what was central to the next steps of the war. The first step was formulating a grand strategy of "closing the ring" around German-dominated territory by opening offensives on several points around the periphery of Europe and North Africa. This would have the advantage of weakening the Germans while the Allies (especially America, which Churchill described as being "half ready" when it entered the war) gathered strength for the main invasion that would not come until 1944. It also set up for the Allies a wide range of choices as to where subsequent offensive action could be directed. True to form, once the

D-Day invasion (code named *Overlord*) was decided upon as the primary course of action, Churchill established a special "Overlord Preparation Committee" that began meeting weekly starting three months before the invasion date.

Factor in Risk and Chance; Keep Things in Proper Proportion

All action in war, and nearly all action in business, involves some degree of risk, and as with all human affairs, the element of chance cannot be eliminated or controlled. "All war is hazard," Churchill wrote after the Dardanelles disaster. "Victory is only wrested by running risks." Churchill was fond of saying that he did not object to chance, but felt it a mistake to be the victim of design.

Churchill always placed a premium on action, so much so that one of his closest aides once described Churchill's policy as "action for action's sake." Churchill understood that institutional inertia, passivity, and collective counsel all tended toward inaction or half-hearted action based on half-measures. "You cannot win this war by sitting still," Churchill wrote in World War I. After David Lloyd-George replaced the passive Herbert Asquith as prime minister in 1916, Churchill told the House of Commons: "What does the nation expect of the new National Government? I am going to answer in one word—action. . . . Action—action, not hesitation; action, not words; action, not agitation." Early in World War II he had the same complaint: "We have never done anything but follow the line of least resistance. That leads only to perdition."

This was a theme he would constantly return to during World War II. "The offensive," he wrote early in the war, "is three or four times as hard as passively enduring from day to day. It therefore requires all possible help in early stages. Nothing is easier than to smother it in its cradle." He criticized the caution of the Committee of Imperial Defense as representing "the maximum of study and the minimum of action." In a letter to a fellow cabinet member in 1940 before he became prime minister, an exasperated Churchill complained: "I have two or three projects moving forward, but all I fear will succumb before the tremendous array of negative arguments and forces. . . . Victory will never be found by taking the path of least resistance." Even after Churchill had been aggressively driving the war as prime minister for more than a year, he complained that the "negative in our counsels in the present time is as 10:1."

It may be supposed from these comments that Churchill's bias in favor of action led him to disregard prudent calculations of risk. This has always been a widespread criticism of Churchill, both during his life and by subsequent historians—and he did not always help his own case. In a speech to the House of Commons in 1916, for example, he described the Dardanelles disaster as "a legitimate war gamble," an unfortunate choice of words that added credence to the criticism that he was reckless.

A closer look will show, however, that Churchill had a method for evaluating risk and factoring in chance, and that he exercised considerable caution in making plans and reaching decisions. One of Churchill's maxims was "It is far better to take too many precautions than too few." He also said that it is better not to act "when one has grave doubts as to the consequences of one's act." His reluctance and hesitation about the proposed D-Day invasion of northern France has often been attributed to his supposed fondness for the alternative of striking at the "soft underbelly" of Europe, but in fact Churchill feared that an invasion against strong German fortifications in northern Europe would be too costly or might lead to a World War I–style stalemate. He often went along with counsels of delay for contemplated actions, so that the situation might be understood more clearly. During the opening days of World War II, when the bombing of Germany was contemplated, Churchill commented in the war cabinet how "finely balanced" were the arguments on both sides of the idea. The British Royal Air Force was still badly inferior to the German Luftwaffe, and any bombing of the German homeland would surely lead to retaliation raids against both Britain and France. When Germany launched its massive invasion of France eight months later, Churchill again argued in favor of delaying the immediate bombing of Germany: "The effect of a 24-hour delay could not make any appreciable difference to the difficulty or danger of the attack, but it might enable a clearer view to be obtained of the situation on land." For one of the few times in Churchill's career, it was his colleagues who were more anxious for immediate action.

Churchill's method of judging risk and chance was best articulated in *The River War*, where he wrote:

> Countless and inestimable are the chances of war. . . . The influence of Fortune is powerfully and continually exerted. In the flickering light of conflict the outlines of solid fact throw on every side vague shadows of possibility. We live in a world of "ifs." "What happened," is singular; "what might have happened," legion. But to try to gauge the influence of this uncertain force were utterly futile, and it is perhaps wise, and indisputably convenient, *to assume that the favorable and adverse chances equate, and then eliminate them both from the calculation.* (Emphasis added.)

In other words, judgment should yield neither to optimism nor to pessimism, but to the realistic mean between the two. "A true sense of proportion must rule," was Churchill's maxim for evaluating the often mixed results of any initiative. "If things never turn out as well as you expect them," he wrote during World War I after an expected disaster was averted, "it is also true that they never turn out as badly." If one has performed "due diligence," so to speak, in the course of making plans and reaching decisions, then Churchill was always confident enough to "take refuge beneath the impenetrable arch of probability." "Sometimes right things turn out wrong," he said in December 1941, "and wrong things turn out right." It was the sense that well-considered actions will average out in the long run that gave Churchill the confidence to make the reflection offered in the epigraph to this chapter: "We have been helped by our mistakes and injured by our most sagacious decisions." The ability "to take the rough with the smooth"—a common Churchill phrase— was what enabled him repeatedly to make tough decisions. This equanimity also enabled him to deal with the frequent crises and setbacks that were part of the natural course of events. "If something went wrong," one of his aides reminisced after the war, "he would patiently start again at the beginning."

Finally, Churchill was always firmly averse to second-guessing. "You cannot be content to sit as a judge pronouncing on events *after* they have taken place," he wrote in 1915.

Change Your Mind in the Presence of New Facts

"I would rather be right than consistent," Churchill said. He not only changed political parties twice, but he changed his mind about a number of issues. In almost every case, he changed his mind, or came to a different perspective about an old opinion, based on what he called "new facts." New facts nearly always lead to change of some kind. Churchill had a rare ability to discern immediately what changes were implied by new facts, and how policy should be adapted to meet the new environment. In the area of technological advance, Churchill was always quick to see how new military inventions or innovations would drastically change battlefield conditions and therefore the entire dynamic of warfare. For example, the torpedo changed the nature of naval blockades—a favorite strategy of maritime Britain—because it made the "close blockade" (where the fleet was literally stationed at the opening of enemy harbors) impossible. When the submarine began coming into its own in the early years of the 20th century, most conventional thinkers regarded it as a *defensive* weapon, to be used primarily to complicate blockades established at a more distant perimeter. But Churchill understood that torpedo-bearing submarines would become powerful *offensive* weapons, operating on the open seas far distant from their home bases. Churchill first put this case to the Committee of Imperial Defense in 1912, where it was not immediately acclaimed.

New facts could also be strategic in nature. For example, when developments in the Balkan nations in 1942 looked to be favoring the Allies and perhaps leading to the entry of Turkey on the side of the Allies, Churchill argued that these new facts required that "the whole position [of Allied strategy] must be completely re-surveyed." "The fact which dominates action" is a typical Churchill formula that appears throughout his speeches and writings. It was the new fact that the navy thought it could reduce the Turkish forts in the Dardanelles from a safe distance that led Churchill to embrace the Dardanelles idea in 1915.

Perhaps the most dramatic new fact that led to a complete change in Churchill's views was the development of nuclear weapons. "The entire foundation of human affairs was revolution-ized and mankind placed in a situation both measureless and laden with doom," Churchill said in 1955. Once the Soviet Union devel-oped its own nuclear capabilities and ended the Anglo-American monopoly on nuclear weapons in the late 1940s, the confrontational, belligerent Churchill of the 1930s gave way to the conciliatory Churchill who served as prime minister in the 1950s. He hoped for summit meeting between himself, President Eisenhower, and Stalin's successors to reach a comprehensive settlement on East-West tensions. Although the summit never took place (much to Chur-chill's disappointment and frustration), his natural optimism still led him to sound a hopeful note in his typically pithy way. "It may well be," he said in one of his last speeches as prime minister in 1955, "that we shall by a sublime irony have reached a stage in this story where safety will be the sturdy child of terror, and survival the twin brother of annihilation."

Churchill's openness to new facts shows his flexibility and adaptability, and provides a corrective to the common view that he was stubborn. Though of course Churchill would argue vigorously for his point of view in cabinet deliberations and elsewhere, it is a mistake to confuse *resolve* with stubbornness. The fact that he so often changed his mind in the presence of new facts, and that he deferred repeatedly to his advisers, absolves him of the charge that he was unreasonably stubborn.

PITFALLS TO AVOID

While Churchill's thought process was a combination of blending a far-seeing imagination for the broad view with attention to the nitty-gritty details, he also had a balanced sense of how it was possible to take this thought process too far. It is from Churchill's list of "don'ts" that it is possible to appreciate how he found his way between the extremes.

Looking Too Far Ahead

"Churchill had trained himself to look ahead," Martin Gilbert wrote. "This had been his method of thought for more than 40 years." But Churchill also emphasized from time to time that "It is a mistake to look too far ahead," adding, "Only one link in the chain of destiny can be handled at a time." "I never look beyond a battle," Churchill wrote during World War I. "It is a culminating event, and like a brick wall bars all further vision."

While Churchill always emphasized that "there must be a design and theme" for all major activities, he also stressed that "It is only with some difficulty and within limits that provision can be made for the future. *Experience shows that forecasts are usually falsified and preparations always in arrears.*" (Emphasis added.) Churchill had learned this lesson the hard way with the Dardanelles fiasco, discussed in Chapter 3. A rereading of the cabinet minutes shows that practically before the echoes of the first shots had died away, the cabinet was gleefully speculating about what kind of territorial settlement would be extracted from the defeated Turks.

One of the tricks of finding the right balance is to have a clear awareness of the relationship between short-term and long-term projects. Two equal and opposite errors are typical: people sacrifice promising short-term projects to a vague long run that never arrives or is continuously postponed, or they allow the long run to get eaten up in an endless series of short-run initiatives that never gel into a coherent long-run strategy. These errors are common to warfare and commerce alike. Churchill faced this "usual clash between short-term and long-term projects" repeatedly in both world wars.

One of Churchill's most frustrating episodes occurred in the early months of World War II, in 1939 and 1940, when he was still First Lord of the Admiralty. At a time when Britain and France were much weaker than Germany but nevertheless looking for a way to take the offensive by some means in some place, the war cabinet pondered an invasion of Norway and northern Sweden to disrupt Germany's iron ore supplies. Churchill pushed this proposal with vigor in the war cabinet, but "every argument had been brought forward in favor of doing nothing." Although war cabinet opinion was generally in favor of the idea, delay after delay occurred in merely planning for the Norway action. Several military advisers argued in favor of different long-range plans instead. Among the objections which aroused Churchill's ire was "the insidious argument, 'don't spoil the big plan for the sake of the small,' when there is really very little chance of the big plan being resolutely attempted." The numerous delays and half-hearted plans proved fatal to the idea, as the Germans consolidated their grip on Norway before the British offensive began. To Churchill's many critics, it seemed like the Dardanelles all over again.

While there is no clear-cut method for deciding the right balance between short and long term, Churchill's emphasis on action and initiative probably provides the right leaven for striking a balance. Churchill was constantly proposing small schemes for immediate action, and even though many of these ideas never came to pass, the constant prodding for action along with his focus on the broad view no doubt caused his colleagues and subordinates to concentrate more closely on both short- and long-term aspects of the war effort.

Excessive Perfectionism

The flip side of the tendency of collective counsels to breed timidity and delay is an excessive perfectionism that has the practical effect of smothering any attempted action. Again Churchill's view presents a paradox or seeming contradiction. He was always probing after details in order to make sure that things "went right," but at the same time he was a fierce critic of perfectionism. In 1942 he wrote: "The maxim 'Nothing avails but perfection' may be spelt shorter, 'Paralysis.'" He also was fond of the commonplace axiom, "Do not let the better be the enemy of the good." Again it is possible to see that Churchill understood this lesson at an early age. He wrote of it in *The River War* in 1898: "All politics are series of compromises and bargains, and while the historian may easily mark what would have been the best possible moment for any great undertaking, a good moment must content the administrator."

Decisions for Decision's Sake or Action for Action's Sake Alone

Just as Churchill exercised restraint in looking too far ahead, he also had a strong sense of when a decision should be deferred or not made at all, especially where a fluid situation might present new facts that would argue for a different decision. One of his top aides from his days as chancellor of the exchequer noted that Churchill "disliked giving snap decisions on cases stated orally." Sir Ian Jacob wrote that "The Prime Minister, curiously enough, was never keen on making decisions on matters that did not require immediate action. Unless one had to be made he liked to discuss the pros and cons at length, and would then adjourn the meeting for further thought, particularly if the decision was likely to be one which went against the grain." There were times when Churchill clearly acted according to the saying, "don't just do something; stand there!"

Churchill often complained that the Foreign Office "never could see when it was wise to do nothing." On another occasion where one of his field commanders faced a minor but unresolvable dilemma, Churchill counseled, "Sometimes there are great advantages in letting things slide for a while." Churchill frequently adopted the tactic of deferring issues that could not be immediately resolved, especially in the wartime summit meetings he held with FDR and Stalin. For example, Churchill argued for putting off decisions about whether to dismember and deindustrialize Germany once it was defeated, knowing that postwar tensions with the Soviet Union might make it in the interest of Western Europe to keep Germany united and economically strong. On this sensitive question Churchill wrote to his foreign minister, Anthony Eden, in early 1945: "Guidance in these mundane matters is granted to us only step by step, or at the utmost a step or two ahead. There is therefore great wisdom in reserving one's decisions as long as possible and until all the facts and forces that will be potent at the moment are revealed." Churchill intended, however, to "have it out" with Stalin at the Potsdam conference that followed the defeat of Germany in 1945. During the early days of that conference, Churchill wrote, "I allowed differences that could not be adjusted either round the table or by the Foreign Ministers at their daily meetings to stand over. A formidable body of questions on which there was disagreement was in consequence piled upon the shelves. . . . I intended . . . to come to grips with the Soviet Government on this catalogue of decisions." But he had to return to England in the middle of the conference, there to learn that he had been voted out of office and would not be returning to the conference table.

It is impossible to climb inside the mind of another and see the thought process actually at work or predict the decision on any given issue. In the case of Churchill, though, it is evident that he was aided in making these close judgments by his heavy reliance on the deliberative counsels of his colleagues and advisers. Contrary to the oft-expressed view that Churchill dominated all meetings with lengthy monologues or even "harangues," in fact he listened closely to his colleagues and advisers and often went round the table soliciting their opinions individually. "It is always a good thing," he wrote to one of his principal deputies, "to collect thoughts from as many quarters as possible."

The crucial difference between councils headed by Churchill and councils headed by others was that Churchill was not a passive equal among equals, as chairs of committees too often tend to be. He was always driving his colleagues toward decision, or to consider the next available alternative, rather than engage in aimless, unfocused musing. One of his many secretaries described his method as follows: "If he summoned anyone to discuss a problem he would throw out a number of alternative solutions. In cases where decisions were outstanding he gave them instantly. . . . He accepted advice provided it was clear and that his advisers were competent to advise." The purpose of many of his proposals, especially his more imaginative and impractical ones, was to stimulate others to use their own imagination and initiative in solving a problem. Above all, Churchill's ability to direct people's attention to the broad view kept deliberations tightly focused. An aide summarized this ability by saying that "Winston is marvelous at picking up all the threads and giving them coherent shape and form."

Churchill understood, finally, that a clear thought process was not only the road to correct decisions, but also to efficiency. When asked in 1941 how long he thought it would take to win the war,

Churchill answered: "If we manage it well, it will only take half as long as if we manage it badly."

———————•◆•———————

THE DO'S AND DON'TS OF CHURCHILL'S THOUGHT PROCESS

• *Always concentrate on the broad view and the central features of the problem at hand.*
Churchill's maxim: "It is a good thing to stand away from the canvas from time to time and take a full view of the picture."

• *Factor in risk and chance by keeping things in proper proportion.*
Churchill's maxim: "Assume that the favorable and adverse chances equate, and then eliminate them both from the calculation."

• *Keep open to changing your mind in the presence of new facts.*
Churchill's maxim: "I would rather be right than consistent."

• *Be careful not to look too far ahead.*
Churchill's maxims: "Only one link in the chain of destiny can be handled at a time." "It is only with some difficulty and within limits that provision can be made for the future. Experience shows that forecasts are usually falsified and preparations always in arrears."

• *Avoid excessive perfectionism.*
Churchill's maxims: "'Nothing avails but perfection' may be spelt shorter, 'Paralysis.'" "Do not let the better be the enemy of the good."

• *Don't make decisions for decision's sake.*
Churchill's maxim: "There is great wisdom in reserving one's decisions as long as possible and until all the facts and forces that will be potent at the moment are revealed."

CHAPTER 7

CHURCHILL THE COMMUNICATOR

———◆◆◆———

Of all the talents bestowed upon men, none is so precious as the gift of oratory.... Abandoned by his party, betrayed by his friends, stripped of his offices, whoever can command this power is still formidable.

—WINSTON S. CHURCHILL, 1897

COMMUNICATION SKILLS ARE rightly rated as the most important skills one can have. Churchill will always be best remembered for his inspiring speeches during Britain's "finest hour" in 1940, when he delivered some of his most memorable phrases— "I have nothing to offer but blood, toil, tears, and sweat," or his tribute to the Royal Air Force: "Never in the field of human endeavor have so many owed so much to so few." CBS News broadcaster Edward R. Murrow aptly summarized Churchill's achievement: "Churchill mobilized the English language," Murrow said, "and sent it into battle."

Churchill's soaring oratory did not come naturally to him, and the lesson of Churchill as a communicator is that communication skills are as much a matter of study, practice, and hard work as any other kind of skill. Churchill suffered from a speech impediment— a slight lisp—that led him as a young man to seek out diction lessons and even to consider radical oral surgery. Though he had an astonishing literal memory—he was able to recite with complete accuracy long poems he had read decades earlier—he never gave a speech from memory. Early in his parliamentary career Churchill went blank in the middle of a speech in the House of Commons and had to sit down in considerable embarrassment, and ever after that faltering moment he thoroughly prepared his speeches ahead of time and always worked from detailed notes when delivering a speech. He often spent several days working on a single speech. He spent six weeks polishing his first major parliamentary speech in 1901. Even at the worst moment of the war crisis in 1940, Churchill said: "I did not begrudge twelve hours preparing a speech to the House of Commons." Many of his famous quips were also premeditated. "Must you fall asleep when I am speaking?" a fellow MP asked him the House of Commons one day. "No, it is purely voluntary," Churchill replied. His close friend Lord Birkenhead once said that "Winston has spent the best years of his life writing impromptu speeches." The main character of Churchill's only novel (*Savrola*, published in 1900), a political figure and orator obviously based on Churchill himself, remarks that "These impromptu feats of oratory existed only in the minds of the listeners; the flowers of rhetoric were hothouse plants."

Both Churchill's prose and his speeches were the product of long study and reflection, beginning early in his life. He burnished his appreciation for the English language through his own extensive reading of English classics, from Shakespeare and the King James Bible to the Victorian poets and historians.

The Scaffolding of Rhetoric

When he was a 24-year-old army officer stationed in India, Churchill wrote a short reflection on "The Scaffolding of Rhetoric" that set out four constructive principles of effective communication—principles that are evident in Churchill's entire career.

The first was *correctness of diction*. "Knowledge of a language is measured by the nice and exact appreciation of words. There is no more important element in the technique of rhetoric than the continual employment of the best possible word," he wrote. Churchill generally eschewed long, multisyllabic words in favor of short words. "The unreflecting often imagine that the effects of oratory are produced by the use of long words," he wrote. "The shorter words of a language are usually the more ancient," and therefore the more widely understood. "All the speeches of great English rhetoricians," he observed, "display an uniform preference for short, homely words of common usage." He used to scorn what he called "those professional intellectuals who revel in . . . polysyllables." "Personally," he added, "I like short words."

Churchill's speeches and writings follow this guide, employing short words and phrases and avoiding jargon or involved construction. Jargon and highfalutin phrases are usually employed to shade meaning, evade clarity, or mask confusion of thought. Churchill's few departures from this practice seem designed for just this purpose. During a controversy in the House of Commons in 1906 over Chinese labor in South Africa, which Churchill's party had criticized as verging on "slave labor" during the previous election campaign, Churchill had to defend a new government policy that critics said did not fulfill the government's pledge to make labor reforms. To say that the government's new policy amounted to a continuation of slave labor would be, Churchill said, to commit a "terminological inexactitude." His phrase caused an uproar in the House. Joseph Chamberlain, in reply, used language that might have come straight from Churchill's "Scaffolding of Rhetoric" meditation: "That is English as she is wrote at the Colonial Office. Eleven syllables, many of them of Latin or Greek derivation, when one good English word, a Saxon word of a single syllable [lie], would do!"

Churchill especially disliked bureaucratic appellations. He constantly demanded simplification of bureaucratese. His most famous simplification was the renaming of the "Local Defense Volunteers" in World War II. He wanted them called the "Home Guard." He kept watch especially against jargon. He protested referring to the poor as the "lower income group," and calling a truck a "commercial vehicle." He dressed down civil servants who would write "The answer is in the affirmative," wondering why they were incapable of a simple "Yes." When the Ministry of Food, responsible for wartime rationing, proposed the establishment of "Communal Feeding Centers," Churchill protested: "I hope the term 'Communal Feeding Centers' is not going to be adopted. It is an odious expression, suggestive of Communism and the workhouse. I suggest you call them 'British Restaurants.' Everybody associates the word 'restaurant' with a good meal and they may as well have the name if they cannot get anything else." When the Labour Party's 1950 housing policy chose the term "accommodation unit" to denote houses and apartments, Churchill, then Leader of the Opposition in the House of Commons, had a field day: "I don't know how we are going to sing our old song 'Home Sweet Home.' 'Accommodation Unit, Sweet Accommodation Unit, there's no place like our Accommodation Unit.' I hope to live to see the British democracy spit all this rubbish from their lips."

Churchill's second principle was *rhythm*. "The great influence of sound on the human brain is well known," he wrote. "The sentences of the orator when he appeals to his art become long, rolling and sonorous. The peculiar balance of the phrases produces a cadence which resembles blank verse rather than prose." As you would expect from someone who enjoyed and memorized a large amount of poetry, Churchill's speeches and writings tended to have a signature cadence. Again, shorter words and phrases lend themselves more easily to this purpose than long, fancy words. Long, fancy words interrupt rhythm, and are the crutch of the underconfident.

Someone once remarked that Churchill was a poet working in prose. A look at the form of his speech notes (which his aides used to refer to as his "psalm form") shows both his attention to rhythm and his poetic imagination. His speaking notes for a 1922 speech are a typical example:

What a terrible disappointment the Twentieth Century
   has been
How terrible & how melancholy
is long series of disastrous events
wh have darkened its first 20 years.
We have seen in ev country a dissolution,
a weakening of those bonds,
a challenge to those principles
a decay of faith
an abridgment of hope
on wh structure & ultimate existence
of civilized society depends.
We have seen in ev part of the globe
one gt country after another
wh had erected an orderly, a peaceful
a prosperous structure of civilized society,
relapsing into hideous succession
into bankruptcy, barbarism or anarchy.

Churchill's third principle was *accumulation of argument.* Nearly all his speeches and writings display this organizing principle. "A series of facts is brought forward all pointing in a common direction," he wrote. "The end appears in view before it is reached." Churchill's long memoranda, even more than his speeches, display a scaffolding in the form of numbered paragraphs that build toward his conclusion.

Churchill's fourth principle is *analogy.* Analogy, he wrote, "appeals to the everyday knowledge of the hearer and invites him to decide the problems that have baffled his powers of reason by the standard of the nursery and the heart." Churchill's use of vivid analogies was second nature to him; a complete collection of his analogic phrases would fill a medium-size book. The beauty of an apt analogy is that it conveys in one or two sentences a truth or insight that is less convincing or clear when explained at more length. The futility and slaughter of trench warfare attrition in World War I, for example, can be amply explained as a function of the superiority of defensive weaponry and tactics available at the time. The artillery barrage and huge manpower needs necessary to mount an offensive against such defenses could not be sustained beyond a short range, making large breakthroughs impossible. Still the commanders on both sides tried over and over again. Churchill explained the frustrating dynamic equilibrium of the war much more effectively: "Every offensive lost its force as it proceeded. *It was like throwing a bucket of water over the floor.* It first rushed forward, then soaked forward, and finally stopped altogether until another bucket could be brought." (Emphasis added.) For another—unrelated but irresistable—example, he described his dislike for golf by saying that it was "like chasing a quinine pill around a cow pasture."

Often it is possible to see all four principles at work in Churchill's speeches as well as his prose. He used short, crisp sentences, laden with analogy and vivid imagery, knit into rhythmic paragraphs in which each sentence built on the previous sentence to a powerful climax. His vivid imagery and carefully crafted language were never finer than during his "Wilderness Years" in the 1930s, as he warned against the growing menace of Nazi Germany. He first warned of the tyrannical and warlike nature of Nazism in the 1920s, before Hitler had become chancellor, and as early as 1932 Churchill described disarmament as "mush, slush, and gush." His warning in 1936 that Britain was passing through "the locust years" was capped with a peroration that perfectly conveyed the sluggishness of government policy:

> Everything, he assured us, is entirely fluid. I am sure that
> that is true. Anyone can see what the position is. The Govern-
> ment simply cannot make up their minds, or they cannot get
> the Prime Minister to make up his mind. So they go on in
> strange paradox, decided only to be undecided, resolved to be

irresolute, adamant for drift, solid for fluidity, all-powerful to
be impotent. So we go on preparing more months and years—
precious, perhaps vital to the greatness of Britain—for the
locusts to eat.

The conclusion to his famous speech after the Munich agreement in
1938, which handed over a portion of Czechoslovakia to Hitler, displays this characteristic tempo and imagery in the highest degree:

I do not begrudge our loyal, brave people, who were ready to
do their duty no matter what the cost, who never flinched under
the strain of last week—I do not grudge them the natural,
spontaneous outburst of joy and relief when they learned that
the hard ordeal would no longer be required of them at the
moment; but they should know the truth. They should know
that there has been gross neglect and deficiency in our defenses;
they should know that we have sustained a defeat without a
war, the consequences of which will travel far with us along
our road; they should know that we have passed a milestone in
our history, when the whole equilibrium of Europe has been
deranged, and that the terrible words have for the time being
been pronounced against the Western democracies: "Thou are
weighed in the balance and found wanting." And do not suppose that this is the end. This is only the beginning of the reck-
oning. This is only the first sip, the first foretaste of a bitter cup
which will be proffered to us year by year unless by a supreme
recovery of moral health and martial vigor, we arise again and
take our stand for freedom as in the olden time.

In addition to his skillful use of climax, Churchill was also prac-
ticed in the art of the dramatic anticlimax, which he usually put to
humorous and frequently disarming effect. During a contentious
debate in the House of Commons following the occasionally violent
general strike of 1924 (during which Churchill supervised the pub-

lication of a much-criticized government newspaper, the *British Gazette*), Churchill taunted his Labour Party critics with the promise: "Make your minds perfectly clear that if you let loose upon us again a general strike, we will loose upon you—[pause]—another *British Gazette*." The House, expecting vitriol and threats of a police crackdown, erupted in laughter at this anticlimax. During World War II, when Churchill heard that a captured German general was to dine with Field Marshall Bernard Montgomery, who had an austere and pompous manner, Churchill remarked: "I sympathize with General von Thoma. Defeated, humiliated, in captivity, and—[pause]—dinner with General Montgomery."

Put It in Writing—and Keep It Short

In addition to his carefully prepared speeches, Churchill's voluminous minutes and memoranda are legendary. They proceeded from a fundamental management principle. In *The World Crisis* Churchill had written, "Nothing of any consequence was done by me by word of mouth," and in *The Second World War* Churchill wrote, "I am a strong believer in transacting official business by *the Written Word*." Hence, a memorandum distributed shortly after Churchill became prime minister set the tone for his administration: "Let it be clearly understood that all directions emanating from me are made in writing, or should be immediately confirmed in writing, and that I do not accept responsibility for matters relating to national defense, on which I am alleged to have given decisions, unless they are recorded in writing." "This was a deliberate attempt," Martin Gilbert explained, "to prevent the chaos that had so often resulted during the First World War following some verbal remark by Asquith, or Lloyd-George, upon which actions were initiated, and then challenged by the Prime Minister as not being what he had asked for."

Churchill not only employed concise writing; he also demanded it of his colleagues. Churchill employed concise English in his own missives. He once gave a copy of Fowler's *Modern English Usage* to the Queen as a Christmas present. There is the oft-told story of Churchill returning a memorandum in which a civil servant had objected to the ending of a sentence with a preposition, to which Churchill noted: "This is the sort of pedantry up with which I will not put." In a memorandum to the Foreign Office during World War II, Churchill complained, "Attention should be drawn to the misspelling 'inadmissable.' I have noticed this several times before in Foreign Office telegrams."

He complained regularly that reports and memoranda were too verbose. "This paper," he complained in cabinet one day, "by its very length defends itself against the risk of being read." "A daily report should be limited to one page, and the weekly report should be a well-digested summary," he instructed in the fall of 1940. Two months later, he wrote in exasperation to his senior aides: "Please look at this mass of stuff which reaches me in a single morning. . . . More and more people must be banking up behind these different papers, the bulk of which defeats their purpose. Try now and simplify, shorten and reduce." "It is sheer laziness not compressing thought into a reasonable space," he complained to one of his secretaries. He lived by what he called "the commandment" to "Say what you have to say as clearly as you can and in as few words as possible." An example of his inclination to brevity can be found in an editorial change he made in the Conservative Party platform of 1950. Churchill shortened "It is our intention to initiate consultations with the Unions" to "We shall consult with the Unions."

Increasingly he stipulated that information he requested should be supplied to him "on a single sheet of paper." A memorandum on "Brevity" that Churchill distributed to his entire war cabinet in August 1940 is worth reproducing in its entirety:

Brevity

MEMORANDUM BY THE PRIME MINISTER

To do our work, we all have to read a mass of papers. Nearly all of them are far too long. This wastes time, while energy has to be spent in looking for the essential points.

I ask my colleagues and their staffs to see to it that their Reports are shorter.

(i) The aim should be Reports which set out the main points in a series of short, crisp paragraphs.

(ii) If a report relies on a detailed analysis of some complicated factors, or on statistics, these should be set out in an Appendix.

(iii) Often the occasion is best met by submitting not a full-dress Report, but an *Aide-memoire* consisting of headings only, which can be expanded orally if needed.

(iv) Let us have an end of such phrases as these: "It is also of importance to bear in mind the following considerations . . .", or "Consideration should be given to the possibility of carrying into effect. . ." Most of these woolly phrases are mere padding, which can be left out altogether, or replaced by a single word. Let us not shrink from using the short expressive phrase, even if it is conversational.

Reports drawn up on the lines I propose may at first seem rough as compared with the flat surface of officialese jargon. But the saving in time will be great, while the discipline of setting out the real points concisely will prove an aid to clearer thinking.

As this memorandum makes clear, Churchill thought that sloppy verbal expression often indicated a sloppy thought process about the matter at hand. This is why one of the most important aspects of the examination process he proposed for the new Naval War Staff in 1911 was to test "their ability to express their views in writing clearly" and "their ability to draft an accurate report on some given subject as briefly as possible without omitting any essential point."

Churchill's frequent grammatical and linguistic corrections of his subordinates were often a means of prodding them to take action. During a visit to Cairo on the eve of a major battle in 1942, Churchill was disturbed to find that the tanks that had been shipped there at great risk were not massed for a large attack. "Because of a shortage of motor transport," was the excuse given. But Churchill had seen large numbers of trucks in the area, so he sent one of his "Action This Day" minutes asking for an inventory of all motor transport in the area and an analysis of how it was being used. He wanted this report in 24 hours. Back came the reply: A "breakdown" of this kind would require at least a week. This was the perfect opening for Churchill. He demanded that the information be provided in the time specified, and threw in some juicy comments on the ambiguity of the word "breakdown" used in this way. Churchill got the result he sought: The plan was changed, and the tanks were massed.

As this example shows, the use of irony and the play on the meaning of words was a favorite device of Churchill's. His keen appreciation for the meaning and proper usage of words was a key to his humor, because his command of the meaning of words enabled him to offer countless jabs and jests in the form of puns. On a memo from his First Lord of the Admiralty Dudley Pound, Churchill once wrote a one-word comment to indicate his disagreement: "Pennywise." When informed by a colonial governor in Africa of the spread of venereal disease among the native population, Churchill replied, "Ah, Pox Britannica!" A charge he liked to make against the socialists was that "The socialist dream is no longer Utopia but Queuetopia."

More important than the clarity of communication conveyed by written messages is the overall effect they had on everyone throughout the government. "This seems now to be a small innovation," Lord Normanbrook wrote after the war, "but it produced at the time a startling effect." His written messages kept everyone on their toes. "The mere fact that he was known to take an active interest in details," Sir Ian Jacob wrote, "kept everyone alert and active." "The positive good achieved by these personal 'Action This Day' Minutes," Lord Bridges wrote, "was that they brought home to all Ministers and Senior Civil Servants and officers of the three Services that everything, great or small, might come under the Prime Minister's eyes, and that everything should be handled with dispatch."

Most important, Churchill's ubiquitous messages had a substantial effect on morale. "It quickened the pace and improved the tone of administration," Lord Normanbrook wrote, "A new sense of purpose and urgency was created as it came to be realized that a firm hand, guided by a strong will, was on the wheel." Churchill occasionally made a direct appeal in writing for his colleagues to keep in mind matters of morale. In the midst of the Dunkirk evacuation in May 1940, Churchill circulated a memorandum to all cabinet members and senior officials that read:

> In these dark days the Prime Minister would be grateful if all
> his colleagues in the Government, as well as high officials,
> would maintain a high morale in their circles; not minimizing
> the gravity of events, but showing confidence in our ability and
> inflexible resolve to continue the war until we have broken the
> will of the enemy to bring all of Europe under his domination.

Although Churchill often used blunt and direct language, he was also the master of softening a message so as to get the point across without giving offense or causing acrimony. One of the best examples of this is his tactful reworking of a telegram to the dominion governments in 1940 regarding the status of the Duke of Windsor. Churchill had been quite close to the Duke when he was King Edward VIII, and had defended him during the abdication crisis in 1936. But the Duke, and especially his American wife Wallace Simpson, were thought to have Nazi sympathies that the Germans might exploit, especially if they remained in Spain or Portugal. The government decided to send the Duke to a sinecure post at one of Britain's overseas colonies. The Colonial Office drafted a message for Churchill to send, which read:

> The activities of the Duke of Windsor on the Continent in recent months have been causing HM [His Majesty] and myself grave uneasiness as his inclinations are well known to be pro-Nazi and he may become the center of intrigue. We regard it as a real danger that he should move freely on the Continent. Even if he were willing to return to this country his presence here would be most embarrassing both to HM and to the Government.
>
> In all the circumstances it has been felt necessary to try to tie him down in some appointment which might appeal to him and his wife and I have decided with HM's approval to offer him the Governorship of the Bahamas. I do not know yet whether he will accept. Despite the obvious objections to this solution we feel that it is the least of possible evils.

Churchill rewrote the message as follows:

> The position of the Duke of Windsor on the Continent in recent months has been causing His Majesty and His Majesty's Government embarrassment, as, though his loyalties are unimpeachable, there is always a backwash of Nazi intrigue which seeks to make trouble about him. The Continent is now in enemy hands. There are personal and family difficulties about his return to this country.
>
> In all the circumstances it has been felt that an appointment abroad might appeal to him and his wife, and I have, with His Majesty's cordial approval, offered him the Governorship of

the Bahamas. His Royal Highness has intimated that he will accept the appointment. I think he may render useful service and find a suitable occupation there.

We should not be fooled by Churchill's extraordinary literary output, or by the fact that he dictated most of his works, into thinking that writing was a matter of ease for him. He would often pause in frustration searching his mind for the right word or phrase, and he would revise extensively. F. Scott Fitzgerald wrote that "All good writing is swimming under water and holding your breath." Like his other skills, Churchill's communication ability was the result of hard work and determined deliberation.

CHURCHILL THE COMMUNICATOR

• *Remember the scaffolding of effective language: diction, rhythm, accumulation of argument, and analogy.*

• *Conduct all important matters in writing.*
Churchill's maxims: "I am a strong believer in transacting official business by *the Written Word*." "Let it be clearly understood that all directions emanating from me are made in writing, or should be immediately confirmed in writing, and that I do not accept responsibility for matters relating to national defense, on which I am alleged to have given decisions, unless they are recorded in writing."

• *Keep messages concise.*
Churchill's maxim: "It is sheer laziness not compressing thought into a reasonable space."

CHAPTER 8

CHURCHILL'S PERSONAL TRAITS

The Completion of Leadership

———◆———

Even ordinary life and business involve the encountering of unknown factors and require some effort of the imagination, some stress of the soul, to overcome them.

—WINSTON S. CHURCHILL, 1922

GOOD WORK HABITS, coherent organizational structures, and superior communication skills do not in and of themselves constitute leadership or guarantee success. Leadership is equally a matter of personal character as of executive skill. Military historian Maxwell Schoenfeld reminds us that even though Churchill's executive reorganization of the war effort after he became prime minister was essential to his success, "The central problem was essentially one of leadership, not of staff."

Churchill learned this lesson early on from his first political patron, Prime Minister Herbert Asquith. Asquith was one of the most dominant and successful politicians of the period, and he led his Liberal Party to several major political triumphs in the years before World War I. He advanced Churchill's career more than any other prime minister. After one of Asquith's political victories, Churchill wrote to him admiringly, "It is not always that a leader's personal force can be felt amid all that turmoil." Years later, looking back after Asquith's death, Churchill wrote: "Mr. Asquith was probably one of the greatest peace-time Prime Ministers we have ever had." The key term here is "peace-time." As noted in Chapter 3, Asquith was not up to the task of wartime leadership. "In war," Churchill wrote of Asquith several years later in *Great Contemporaries*, "he had not those qualities of resource and energy, of prevision and assiduous management, which ought to reside in the executive. . . . [The war] demanded a frenzied energy at the summit; an effort to compel events rather than to adjudicate wisely and deliberately upon them."

What made possible Churchill's own "frenzied energy at the summit" was a combination of character traits that transcend mere executive skills.

Courage and Optimism

Churchill's courage was evident from his earliest days as a young lieutenant in the army. Maurice Hankey, cabinet secretary during World War I, wrote later that "We owed a good deal in those early days to the courage and inspiration of Winston Churchill who, undaunted by difficulties and losses, set an infectious example to those of his colleagues who had given less thought than he, if indeed any thought at all, to war problems. . . . His stout attitude did something to hearten his colleagues." After Churchill left the war cabinet for the front line trenches in France, Hankey lamented in his diary: "Since Churchill left the Cabinet and the War Council we have lacked courage more than ever."

The key to Churchill's courage was his unbounded optimism. Only an optimist can be courageous, because courage depends on hopefulness that dangers and hazards can be overcome by bold and risky acts. "I am one of those," he remarked in 1910, "who believe that the world is going to get better and better." He deprecated negative thinking. In a speech to his officers in the trenches in France in 1916, Churchill exhorted: "Laugh a little, and teach your men to laugh. . . . If you can't smile grin. If you can't grin keep out of the way till you can."

"It is a crime to despair," he wrote after the disaster of the Munich agreement in 1938. "It is the hour, not for despair, but for courage and re-building; and that is the spirit which should rule us in this hour." In his last major speech as prime minister in 1955, surveying the growing threat nuclear weapons posed to the very survival of civilization, Churchill concluded: "Meanwhile, never flinch, never weary, never despair."

"All will come right" was a favorite phrase. He repeated it often in the darkest days of World War II, and he seldom ended a wartime speech without a ringing note of optimism, usually drawn or adapted from a famous English poet. (He ended one speech with a lyric from Arthur Hugh Clough: "But westward, look, the land is bright!") After Churchill had been hit by a car and nearly killed in 1931, he summed up his optimism into a credo: "Live dangerously; take things as they come; dread naught, all will be well." "When you get to the end of your luck," he wrote in the 1930s, "there is a comfortable feeling that you have got to the bottom."

Optimism is also the key to the can-do spirit, to the don't-take-no-for-an-answer attitude that is essential to successful executive leadership. Nearly all human organizations are subject to an inertia that results in an it-can't-be-done attitude. This was always unacceptable to Churchill. "Churchill's supreme talent," one of his aides recalled, "was in goading people into giving up their cherished reasons for not doing anything at all." When apprised of delays in shipbuilding in 1939, for example, Churchill sent a memorandum to one of his senior administrators: "It is no use the contractors saying it cannot be done. I have seen it done when full pressure is applied, and every resource and contrivance utilized." And Churchill once urged a diplomat in a cable: "Continue to pester, nag and bite. Demand audiences. Don't take NO for an answer."

Churchill's optimism and cheerfulness tend to be obscured by the accounts of his occasional depression, what he called his "black dog." There is no doubt that the pressures of office and the fearfulness of events often left Churchill profoundly discouraged—especially when he was out of office and powerless to affect events that he understood so clearly. But these occasional collapses of

Churchill's spirit have probably been exaggerated (along with the popular image of his drinking), and in most cases they were short-lived. It is worth noting that Churchill often turned to his favorite hobby—painting—when he was discouraged, but that unlike serious manic depressives or brooding artists who paint dark scenes or write morose poetry, Churchill always painted in bright, vivid colors, a reflection of an underlying optimism and happiness of soul. (Regarding his choice of colors for painting, Churchill wrote: "I rejoice with the brilliant ones, and am genuinely sorry for the poor browns.")

One aspect of his optimism that was especially important was his legendary sense of humor. But this, too, had a serious under-pinning in his mind. "It is my belief," Churchill said, "that you can-not deal with the most serious things in the world unless you also understand the most amusing."

Kindness, Magnanimity, and Gratitude

Like any ambitious, demanding person in a position of great respon-sibility and facing enormous pressures, Churchill could be abrupt and hard on his subordinates. "It is a wonder any of my colleagues are speaking to me," he once remarked during an especially diffi-cult period early in World War II. But as with the accounts of his occasional depression, accounts of Churchill's domineering manner or rudeness have been exaggerated, and his kindness and consideration for his subordinates overlooked.

"The idea that he was rude, arrogant, and self-seeking is entirely wrong," wrote General Ismay, one of his closest aides during the war. Martin Gilbert, who interviewed nearly all Churchill's secre-taries and assistants in the course of research for his massive biog-raphy, wrote: "The overriding impression that his secretaries gave me was of a man who worked hard himself, drove them equally hard, but did so with humor and kindness, alert to their personal needs and quick to apologize for any outburst of anger." The many dairies, memoirs, and other records of experiences with Churchill are replete with observations similar to this account from Lord Normanbrook: "He would at intervals find time to say or write a few words of appreciation which showed a quite exceptional generosity and kindness."

Churchill also was an exceptionally forgiving person—an aspect of magnanimity. "I do not harbor malice," he wrote in a letter in 1921. "I always forgive political attacks or ill-treatment not directed at private life." This trait was most on display after World War II began, when Churchill's position was unassailable on account of his clear and consistent warnings over the previous years. If anyone had a right to say "I told you so" and demand retribution against the position and careers of the officials who had been derelict in their leadership, it was Churchill. But he did no such thing. From a Conservative Party official who had even tried to remove Churchill from Parliament just a few months before the outbreak of war, Churchill most graciously accepted an apology, writing: "I certainly think that Englishmen ought to start fair with one another from the outset in so grievous a struggle and so far as I am concerned the past is dead."

His largest magnanimity was reserved for Neville Chamberlain, the architect of the disastrous Munich agreement with Hitler that Churchill had so bitterly criticized. Chamberlain worked assiduously to keep Churchill out of office in the months and years before war came, and when waning political support compelled his resignation in May 1940, he was not enthusiastic about Churchill replacing him as prime minister. But once Churchill was in the government, Churchill was extremely loyal and supportive of Chamberlain, and after Churchill became prime minister, he defended Chamberlain against critics. (Churchill had kept Chamberlain in the government as a member of the war cabinet.) John Colville noted in his diary that Churchill "never countenances a word against Chamberlain." When a group of MPs demanded a parliamentary "inquest" against those responsible for the conduct of policy before the war (meaning chiefly Chamberlain), Churchill spoke out forcefully against the idea. "This," he said to the House, "would be a foolish and pernicious process. . . . Of this I am quite sure, that if we open a quarrel between the past and the present, we shall find that we have lost the future." Churchill's final kindness to Chamberlain was his eulogy in the House of Commons after Chamberlain's death of cancer in November 1940. Churchill sought to put their past disagreements in the most generous light possible without ignoring them entirely:

> It fell to Neville Chamberlain in one of the supreme crises of the world to be contradicted by events, to be disappointed in his hopes, and to be deceived and cheated by a wicked man. But what were these hopes in which he was disappointed? What were these wishes in which he was frustrated? What was that faith that was abused? They were surely among the most noble and benevolent instincts of the human heart—the love of peace, the toil for peace, the strife for peace, the pursuit of peace, even at great peril, and certainly to the utter disdain of popularity of clamor. Whatever else history may or may not say about these terrible, tremendous years, we can be sure that Neville Chamberlain acted with perfect sincerity according to his lights and strove to the utmost of his capacity and authority, which were powerful, to save the world from the awful, devastating struggle in which we are now engaged. This alone will stand him in good stead as far as what is called the verdict of history is concerned.

It was Churchill's kindness, his sincere interest in people, and his magnanimity that enabled him to win people over consistently. The historian George Dangerfield recounts a typical scene in which Churchill's benign countenance won someone over. "He [a skeptical union worker] and his colleagues had come to think of Mr. Churchill as a modern Nero, with an awful lust for gore; but no— 'the bloodthirsty one looked as lamblike and as amiable as the gentlest shepherd on earth. . . . If patience and courtesy, if anxious effort and sincerity count for respect, then Winston Churchill is entitled as a man to gratitude.' " Another embattled union leader echoed this theme in a memoir of his first meeting with Churchill: "I had formed an opinion of Winston Churchill as a daring, reckless, swashbuckler individual who was afraid of no one. . . . I expected arrogance, military precision, abruptness. When he appeared, I knew I was wrong. He came in, his fresh face all smiles, and greeted me simply, without a trace of side or trappings. I felt I had found a friend."

The most remarkable example of Churchill's magnanimity was his refusal to criticize the British people when they voted him out of office in a landslide just two months after the war ended in 1945. When a colleague spoke to Churchill of the "ingratitude" of the people as the votes were coming in on election night, Churchill replied: "Oh no, I wouldn't call it that. They have had a very hard time." In his resignation message, he said "It only remains for me to express to the British people, for whom I have acted in these perilous years, my profound gratitude for the unflinching, unswerving support which they have given me during my task, and for the many expressions of kindness which they have shown towards their servant." Though Churchill was bitterly disappointed and discouraged, he summoned up his typical good humor when speaking of the blow. When the King offered Churchill a knighthood shortly after the election loss, he declined the honor, saying: "I could not accept the Order of the Garter from my Sovereign when I had received the order of the boot from his people."

Independent Judgment and Self-Criticism

Because Churchill was an excellent talker and master of argument, it is too often supposed that he was not a good listener and did not take criticism well. He was thought to be stubborn, though it should be recognized that stubbornness is the twin of determination, and therefore requires to be kept in proportion. In fact, an important part of Churchill's method and success was his independent judgment and self-criticism. "Every night," he remarked to one of his aides during the war, "I try myself by Court Martial to see if I have done anything effective during the day. I don't mean just pawing the ground, anyone can go through the motions, but something really effective."

Although Churchill's supreme self-confidence always led him to believe he could persuade his colleagues about the course of action he favored, he always sought criticism and advice from his colleagues and subordinates. One of his aides at the Treasury in the 1920s said of Churchill that "He always took criticism very, very meekly. One could say exactly what one liked in the way of criticism. . . . He wanted the full critical value from subordinates."

After setting out his ideas in memoranda to his staff, it was typical of Churchill to conclude with the request: "By all means confront me with the facts and put the worst complexion on figures." On his first day back at the Admiralty in 1939, Churchill sent his initial thoughts to the senior staff with the concluding wish: "The First Lord submits these notes to his naval colleagues for consideration, *for criticism and correction*, and hopes to receive proposals for action in the sense desired." (Churchill's emphasis.)

In a speech to the nation early in the war about the government's war policy, Churchill declared that "We do not shrink from fair criticism. . . . Criticism in the body politic is like pain in the human body. It is not pleasant, but where would the body be without it?" In World War I, he had written that "the object [of parliamentary deliberation] is to find out what is the best thing to do, and counsel and criticism are necessary processes to that end."

Despite Churchill's tendency to dominate meetings with his volubility, he always encouraged a complete discussion of issues, and never penalized or fired anyone from openly or vigorously disagreeing with him. "Opportunity was always given for full dis-cussion," one of his wartime aides wrote. Lord Bridges wrote after the war, "I cannot recollect a single Minister, serving officer or civil servant who was removed from office because he stood up to Churchill and told Churchill that he thought his policy or proposals were wrong." Moreover, Churchill never overruled the service chiefs of staff, even when he strenuously disagreed with their decisions.

Churchill's own self-criticism and independence of judgment, combined with his habit of seeking advice and criticism, led him to change his mind from time to time. As noted earlier, he once said—and meant—"I would rather be right than consistent." The same dominating purpose usually reveals itself in Churchill's positions; typically he was changing his mind about *means* rather than *ends*. But because he changed his mind and even his party affiliation on two occasions, he set out his thoughts at length in an essay titled "Consistency in Politics":

> A Statesman in contact with the moving current of events and anxious to keep the ship of state on an even keel and steer a steady course may lean all his weight now on one side and now on the other. His arguments in each case when contrasted can be shown to be not only very different in character, but contra-dictory in spirit and opposite in direction: yet his object will throughout have remained the same. . . . We cannot call this in-consistency. In fact it may be claimed to be the truest consis-tency. . . . A Statesman should always try to do what he believes is best in the long view for his country, and he should not be dissuaded from so acting by having to divorce himself from a great body of doctrine to which he formerly sincerely adhered.

Loyalty to the Team

Throughout his life and after Churchill has suffered from the repu-tation of being an overly ambitious glory-seeker. It is a charge that he himself would not necessarily dispute. He disliked sharp party partisanship, and his rugged independence led him to switch parties twice, infuriating many of his fellow MPs.

This fierce independence of opinion and loose allegiance to party led many to consider him unreliable and disloyal. While this judgment is reasonably well-founded as it applies to Churchill the independent politician, a closer look will show that during periods when he held a responsible high office, Churchill was extremely loyal and supportive of his colleagues and superiors—he was a genuine team player. Throughout his "Wilderness Years" in the 1930s, even as his party leadership snubbed him and turned a disdainful ear to his advice, he campaigned vigorously on behalf of the Conservative Party during general elections.

Once a policy was arrived at or a political quarrel decisively settled, Churchill would cease his criticism or opposition and get on board. After losing a long and often bitter fight against the India dominion policy in the early 1930s, Churchill told one of his opponents that "you need not expect anything but silence or help from us." He was fond of quoting the words of Lord Cranborne, who had opposed the Reform Bill of 1867: "It is the duty of every Englishman, and of every English party to accept a political defeat cordially, and to lend their best endeavors to secure the success, or to neutralize the evil, of the principles to which they have been forced to succumb."

Because of Churchill's formidable speaking skills, his cabinet colleagues often relied on him to assume the burden of defense against criticism in the House of Commons. This he always did with vigor and usually with success, even when he was not in full agreement with the cabinet policy or when the policy clashed with his own previously expressed opinions on the issue.

Rest, Relaxation, and Change of Pace

Churchill is reported to have said once that "There is no good time for a vacation, so take one anyway." Churchill was the master of the working vacation. Churchill took many long trips, both in and out of office. He seldom took a trip that was complete leisure, even when he was out of office. "My work and my holidays are the same," he wrote to George Bernard Shaw. He would always take along trunkloads of work, usually materials for his current book project. During World War II he would spend nearly every weekend at the prime minister's country retreat, Chequers (the British equivalent of Camp David).

The importance of recreation for Churchill was not so much to find rest from his preoccupations as it was to stimulate his mind through a change of pace. "Human beings do not require rest," he once remarked to an aide. "What they require is change, or else they become bloody-minded." He elaborated on this theme in his essay "Painting as a Pastime," which described how he took up painting in the months immediately after his dismissal from the Admiralty in 1915—a period of profound stress and disappointment for him. Churchill quickly became as proficient as an artist as he was as a writer, though he was bashful about exhibiting his paintings. (Pablo Picasso is reported to have said of Churchill's painting: "If that man were a painter by profession he would have no trouble in earning a good living.") For the rest of his life Churchill derived profound relief through painting, though he only found time to work on one painting during World War II. "If it weren't for painting," he remarked in 1955 shortly after resigning from his second premiership at the age of 80, "I couldn't live; I couldn't bear the strain of things."

"Change is the master key," he wrote. "A man can wear out a particular part of his mind by continually using it and tiring it, just in the same way as he can wear out the elbows of his coat. . . . Change is an essential element in diversion of all kinds." The remedy—change—is supplied through hobbies. "To be really happy and really safe, one ought to have at least two or three hobbies, and they must be real," Churchill wrote. Churchill's other great hobby was bricklaying; he built a large brick wall substantially by himself at Chartwell, his country home.

Churchill's reliance on changes of pace explains in part his unusual work habits. In addition to the change of pace afforded by travels, the various aspects of his daily routine—dictating in bed in the morning, taking naps and baths, working late after dinner—all ensured that each working day would have several different phases. "For every purpose of business or pleasure, mental or physical," he wrote in *My Early Life*, "we ought to break our days and our marches into two." This was why he held almost unfailingly to his afternoon nap. When an American executive told Churchill that his office routine consisted of the regular 8 to 5:30 day in the office, five days a week, Churchill replied: "My dear man, you don't mean it. That is the most perfect prescription for a short life that I've ever heard." He went on to advise the executive about the virtues of a regular nap: "Don't think you will be doing less work because you sleep during the day. That's a foolish notion held by people who have no imagination. You will be able to accomplish more. You get two days in one—well, at least one and a half, I'm sure. When the war started, I *had* to sleep during the day because it was the only way I could cope with my responsibilities."

Calmness under Stress

Churchill was no stranger to the number one problem faced by all executives—stress. Churchill's colleagues and friends marveled at how calm he was amid the most trying circumstances. In part his ability to deal with stress and trial was a function of his courage and fearlessness. He would, for example, set up his painting easel near the front line trenches in World War I, and paint away as shells were exploding nearby. He would seldom duck when shells exploded, sensibly observing that by the time you hear the report of an exploding shell, it is too late to duck. It was this innate courage that enabled him to gather strength in a crisis. Though all Churchill's colleagues said that he held up to the stress of the war extremely well, he was not immune to the effects of stress. Churchill suffered two heart attacks during World War II, and nearly died from pneumonia as well.

There is no silver-bullet solution for stress, of course. Churchill's main method for dealing with stress was *never to be in a hurry*. Churchill could have invented the slogan, "Never let 'em see you sweat." Certainly he epitomized this popular axiom. "Winston's disregard of time," one of his top aides wrote, "is sublime." Churchill's calmness amid commotion and crisis not only imparted confidence to his colleagues and subordinates, but was also the key to his enormous productivity and concentration. One of his secretaries wrote: "I do admire the unhurried way in which he gets through such a colossal amount of work, and yet never seems otherwise than at leisure."

The lesson of Churchill's extraordinary calm and aversion to haste is that hastiness dilutes your concentration, disrupts your priorities, and makes it impossible to follow a consistent method of work. Churchill's calmness and seeming leisure were closely related to his immense powers of concentration, and were in many ways the linchpin of his success.

Personal Contact

Much is made these days of MBWA—Management By Walking Around. Churchill was a relentless practitioner of the idea. He not only valued the face-to-face contact that visiting the scene provided, but it was also a means of gathering unfiltered information firsthand.

Visiting the scene was a practice that dated from Churchill's earliest days, and was perhaps an extension of his first career as a war correspondent. As under-secretary for the colonies, he undertook a tour of Britain's African colonies, reporting back directly to the King about what he found. As home secretary, he toured prisons, which few home secretaries had done before him. As First Lord of the Admiralty from 1911 to 1915, he visited more ships and naval facilities than any First Lord before or since. Between 1911 and the outbreak of World War I, Churchill made 26 trips on the Admiralty yacht *Enchantress*, visiting more than 50 ships as well as numerous harbor and shipyard facilities. His habit of arranging interviews with junior officers and enlisted personnel was not always welcomed by the top brass, but it served Churchill's purpose of gathering information through nonbureaucratic channels and forming his own view of the details of operations. "He had a yarn with nearly all the lower deck men of the ship's company," the *Daily Express* newspaper wrote of a submarine visit in 1912, "asking why, wherefore, and how everything was done. All the sailors 'go the bundle' on him, because he makes no fuss and takes them by surprise. He is here, there, everywhere." As minister of munitions during World War I, Churchill went to France so often—13 times over the last year of the war—that he eventually established an office for himself in Paris.

As prime minister he visited munitions and aircraft factories, shipyards, airfields, radar stations, command posts, front-line coastal defenses, and everything in between. In addition, his foreign travels added up to more than 200,000 miles by the end of the war. His travels stand in sharp contrast to those of his predecessors. Herbert Asquith in World War I never visited his French allies or the commanders and troops in France. Neville Chamberlain during the first year of World War II made very few visits to the allies in France, and paid few visits to war-making facilities on the home front. Churchill's trips, on the other hand, had the tonic effect of rallying morale wherever he went, as well as providing him a window on the war not available from 10 Downing Street.

Face Bad News Squarely and Candidly

Throughout his career, Churchill always believed that bad news should be faced directly and acknowledged candidly to the public. His father's famous motto had been "Trust the people." Churchill would echo this sentiment at many points in his career. In this respect Churchill once again ran against the grain of ordinary political practice, which he once aptly described as "The habit of saying smooth things and uttering pious platitudes and sentiments to gain applause, without relation to the underlying facts." On the contrary, Churchill advised, "Tell the truth to the British people. They are a tough people, a robust people. They may be a bit offended at the moment, but if you have told them exactly what is going on you have insured yourself against complaints and reproaches which are very unpleasant when they come home on the morrow of some disillusion." It was a mistake, he often argued, "to shrink from stating the true facts to the public."

This is an aspect of Churchill's realism, which was always in equipoise to his idealism and optimism. When faced with mounting criticism about the poor progress of the war in early 1942, Churchill demanded a formal vote of confidence debate in the House of Commons to force the issue. "It is because things have gone badly, and worse is to come," he said, "that I demand a Vote of Confidence." Churchill prevailed, by a vote of 464 to 1. Churchill would confront two more confidence motions in the House during the course of the war, each time winning by large margins precisely because of his candor and forcefulness.

He also liked to deliver bad news personally, not only war news to the House of Commons, but to the Allies as well. One of the toughest moments of the war for him was when it became apparent that a second front against the Germans in France could not be opened up in 1943, as had been promised to Marshall Stalin. Churchill decided to go to Moscow to tell Stalin personally: "It was like taking a lump of ice to the North Pole," Churchill said.

CHURCHILL'S PERSONAL TRAITS

- *Optimism.*
Churchill's maxims: "Laugh a little, and teach your men to laugh. . . . If you can't smile grin. If you can't grin keep out of the way till you can." "It is a crime to despair." "Live dangerously; take things as they come; dread naught, all will be well."

- *Kindness, magnanimity, and gratitude.*
Churchill's maxim: "I do not harbor malice. I always forgive political attacks or ill-treatment not directed at private life."

- *Independent judgment and self-criticism.*
Churchill's maxims: "Every night I try myself by Court Martial to see if I have done anything effective during the day." "Criticism . . . is like pain in the human body. It is not pleasant, but where would the body be without it?"

- *Loyalty as a team player.*

- *Rest, relaxation, and change of pace.*
Churchill's maxims: "There is never a good time for a vacation, so take one anyway." "To be really happy and really safe, one ought to have at least two or three hobbies." "For every purpose of business or pleasure, mental or physical, we ought to break our days and our marches into two."

- *Calmness under stress.*

- *Preference for personal contact.*

- *Ability to face bad news squarely.*
Churchill's maxims: "Trust the people, tell the truth." "It is a mistake to shrink from stating the true facts to the public."

CHAPTER 9

CHURCHILL THE INVENTOR AND INNOVATOR

———◆◆◆———

There are plenty of good ideas if only they can be backed with power and brought into reality.

—WINSTON S. CHURCHILL,
LETTER TO ARTHUR CONAN DOYLE, 1917

CHURCHILL WAS A great innovator. He produced a constant stream of ideas for inventions, some impractical but many both useful and realistic—often unconventional but always imaginative. He was the father of naval aviation, and if it cannot be fully said that he was the father of the tank, he was at least its uncle. He found science endlessly fascinating. "We know enough," he wrote in 1932, "to be sure that the scientific achievements of the next fifty years will be far greater, more rapid and more surprising, than those we have already experienced." His imagination led him to foresee the enormous destructive power of the atomic bomb, for example, nearly 20 years before it was invented.

Churchill's subordinates and colleagues often found his fascination with innovation exasperating. More than one good idea of his got labeled "Churchill's folly." On one occasion he delayed the beginning of a war cabinet meeting at a moment of high crisis to present a model of an antiaircraft homing rocket—an early version of the surface-to-air missile. "Do you think this is time for showing off toys?" one minister complained to a colleague.

Part of Churchill's purpose was to stimulate his colleagues to use their imaginations and to spur them to action. One of his aides from the Home Office described his method: "Once a week or oftener Mr. Churchill came to the office bringing with him some adventurous or impossible projects; but after half an hour's discussion something was evolved which was still adventurous but not impossible."

Like all innovators, Churchill repeatedly had to overcome the usual organizational resistance to change—the not-invented-here syndrome. But innovation is most needed in times of rapidly changing circumstances. Overcoming resistance to change and innovation requires a full measure of forcefulness by a leader. Churchill's career provides many examples of innovation in the face of resistance.

Churchill's most successful period of innovation came during his first stint at the Admiralty from 1911 to 1915. His innovations here were of two kinds—technological and organizational. As Chapter 4 noted, Churchill was skillful at restructuring existing organizations, but from time to time he also imposed entirely new organizational schemes. At the Admiralty, he realized that the time had come to institute a Naval War Staff. In addition, he modernized the British fleet, promoted the development of the Naval Air Corps, and drove the development of the tank during World War I. This chapter tells the story of these innovations, and the resistance and challenges Churchill faced in bringing these innovations to reality.

Creating the Naval War Staff

Early on at the Admiralty, Churchill could see that the conditions of modern warfare were changing the way navies would operate in the future. It would not be enough for the navy just to blockade enemy ports and hold off invasion of the home island. In future conflicts, the navy would often be called upon to work in harmony with the army on combined offensive operations. This required a higher level of strategic planning and command over the navy. For this task, Churchill realized that the navy needed a general planning staff similar to the general staff that had long existed for the army.

The senior officers in the navy opposed the creation of a Naval War Staff. Sir Arthur Wilson, the First Sea Lord (equivalent to the American chief of naval operations) at the time Churchill became First Lord, argued that "The agitation for a Naval War Staff is an attempt to adapt to the Navy a system which was primarily designed for an army. . . . The Service would have the most supreme contempt for any body of officers who professed to be specially trained to think." But Wilson was set to retire in just a few months, so although Churchill fully intended to create the Naval War Staff, and had already thought through how it should be constructed, he decided to postpone action until Wilson's departure. Churchill wrote to the prime minister less than a month after taking office at the Admiralty: "I like Sir Arthur Wilson personally & should be very sorry to run the risk of embittering relations which are now pleasant. I therefore propose to take no public action during his tenure."

When Wilson retired five months later as planned, Churchill named Prince Louis of Battenburg (father of Louis Mountbatten) to be the new First Sea Lord. The plan for the creation of a Naval War Staff went forward. In a series of memoranda Churchill set out the case for a Naval War Staff along with a structural outline for such a staff. It is here that Churchill's strong historical imagination can be seen at work once again. The new and rapidly changing conditions of modern warfare, and the closer integration between the fighting services that such warfare would entail, required more sophisticated strategic planning by the highest levels of the military branches. Naval action could no longer be carried on without the forethought of trained experts. As Churchill looked back, he could see that British naval history was marked by a complete absence of any continuity in Admiralty strategic policy. "The technical training for war in the seagoing fleet of today is extremely good," he noted in his first memorandum on the issue. "But it would only be by chance that it was used to the fullest advantage upon a sound prearranged strategic plan." Churchill then made his argument for the necessity of historical reflection:

The small number of officers employed upon the preparation of war plans at the British Admiralty have received no systematic training whatever in the broad strategic principles which all historians agree in emphasizing as permanent in their application, or in the general tendency of the foreign politics of the day, or in the substance of the various treaties and agreements with other Powers which affect or limit our freedom of action as a belligerent, or our rights as a neutral. Service in the Fleet affords no more instruction on these important questions than service in a city office, and no other form of instruction is afforded. Only war itself, or the historical study of war can teach what results or effects may be expected from any particular variety of war policy such as blockade, attacks upon commerce, interruptions of lines of communication, or descents upon territory, and neither of these methods of instruction is open to our naval officers at the present day unless by private and unencouraged effort.

Churchill wrote later in *The World Crisis* that he felt chagrined that "The Royal Navy had made no important contribution in naval history," and that "The standard work on Sea Power was written by an American Admiral [Admiral Mahan]." Britain "had more captains of ships than captains of war."

In addition to the reasons *why* a war staff should be formed, Churchill also had specific thoughts about *how* such a staff should operate (including an organizational chart). In a second memorandum Churchill set out an organizational scheme whose unified structure would become a model for most of his future administrative efforts, especially during World War II:

A proper Staff, whether naval or military, should comprise three main branches, namely, a branch to acquire the information on which action may be taken; a branch to deliberate on the facts so obtained in relation to the policy of the State, and to report thereupon; and thirdly, a branch to enable the final decision of superior authority to be put into actual effect. The War Staff at the Admiralty will, in pursuance of this principle, be organized from the existing elements, in three Divisions: the Intelligence Division, the Operations Division, and the Mobilization Division. These may be shortly described as dealing with War Information, War Plans, and War Arrangements respectively. The Divisions will be equal in status, and each will be under a Director who will usually be a Captain of standing. The three Divisions will be combined under a Chief of Staff.

Churchill succeeded in setting this new scheme into motion, and though it was still somewhat embryonic when World War I began two and a half years later, the Naval War Staff became a permanent feature of the Admiralty.

Converting the Fleet to Oil

Churchill's second major innovation at the Admiralty was the conversion of the navy's principal fuel from coal to oil. Oil-fired ships were faster and had a longer range than coal-fired ships. The fuel conversion would enable the construction of a new generation of faster, better-armored battleships. Churchill not only wanted faster ships, he also wanted to equip them with larger guns. (The current generation of battleships had 13.5-inch guns; a 15-inch gun could fire a shell nearly twice the size of a 13.5-inch gun, and could fire shells a longer distance. This is one of the factors that led Churchill to call his chapter in *The World Crisis* on this issue "The Romance of Design.") But the issue was not as simple as this. England had coal in abundance, but precious little oil. This meant that oil supplies would have to be obtained from great distances overseas, and a large reserve would have to be stored. Oil supplies might be easily disrupted in wartime, or constricted by the foreign owners. "To commit the Navy irrevocably to oil was indeed 'to take arms against a sea of troubles,'" Churchill wrote. Churchill sought to solve this problem by having the government purchase a majority interest in the Anglo-Persian Oil Company in 1913. This acquisition actually generated a substantial revenue for the government in the years ahead.

Perhaps more important than these particular measures was Churchill's vigorous fight to expand naval shipbuilding in response to the rapid German naval buildup. Having argued against naval expenditure in 1909, Churchill in 1913 fought a ferocious battle in the cabinet for increased naval spending. He felt it was vital to maintain a large margin of naval superiority. This controversy led to a breach between himself and his close friend David Lloyd-George (at that time chancellor of the exchequer), and Churchill nearly resigned in the midst of the struggle. In the end, he won the funds he sought.

These and other measures assured Britain's naval supremacy when war came in 1914. Despite enormous effort and expenditure on the part of the Germans to build up a formidable navy over the preceding ten years, the German navy mostly kept to its home waters for the duration of the war, and the allied blockade of Germany, despite the submarine menace, was highly effective.

The Royal Naval Air Service

Churchill's third initiative at the Admiralty was the founding of the Royal Naval Air Service. The invention of the airplane fascinated Churchill. As noted earlier, Churchill had urged the government to send a mission to America to meet the Wright brothers. His enthusiasm for flight led him to take flying lessons, and he even contemplated obtaining a pilot's license until—following the death of his flight instructor in a crash—Churchill's family and friends prevailed upon him to give up this risky adventure. Once again Churchill was arguably exceeding the mandate of his department and poaching on territory that rightly belonged to another department—what had planes to do with the navy was not an unreasonable question at this primitive moment in aviation history. The War Office, in fact, objected to Churchill's designs for an air division at the Admiralty, but admitted that they had no plans to develop aviation themselves. So Churchill persevered, continuing to fight for the idea even though the Treasury turned down his funding request three times. Churchill finally prevailed, and his interest in this new service branch extended to every detail, including the pilots' uniform, the design of landing strips, and even the flaws in the controls of early airplane models. He envisioned the development of the seaplane, and as early as 1914 proposed the idea of the aircraft carrier.

The Development of the Tank

Churchill could immediately see the futility and horrendous slaughter of trench warfare, and he turned his mind to possible alternatives to sending the army "to chew barbed wire in Flanders." As early as six weeks into the war, Churchill inquired about the possibility of some kind of mechanical device to overcome trench defenses, and he had gone ahead and modified several naval automobiles into crude armored cars. Churchill contemplated the development of what he initially called a "land ship." A staff member in charge of research at the Admiralty had proposed developing an armored cross-country car that would carry guns and would be able to surmount obstacles such as trenches and barbed wire. "As we could not go round the trenches," he wrote in *The World Crisis*, "it was evidently necessary to go over them." Again on his own initiative, Churchill allocated Admiralty funds and formed a "Land Ship Committee" within the Admiralty to move the idea forward. "The matter," Churchill wrote later, "was entirely outside the scope of my own Department or of any normal powers which I possessed." To misdirect anyone who might see the plans or a prototype for this experimental weapon, they were to be called "water-carriers for Russia." But the mildly embarrassing abbreviation this offered up—"WCs for Russia"—led to the name being changed to *water-tanks*, and shortly just *tanks*. The development of the tank began as a navy project!

Churchill understood immediately that the tank could make a decisive difference, and offered the best possibility for changing battlefield conditions. But the development of the tank did not get fully under way until after Churchill had left the Admiralty in May 1915. There was no one of prominence remaining in the government who understood the potential significance of the tank, or to advocate its full development and deployment. In fact, the new leadership at the Admiralty wanted to scrap the tank project. Churchill urged his former colleagues to produce tanks in large numbers as quickly as possible. He ran into the usual skepticism about innovation. Even some of his colleagues at the Admiralty referred to the project as "Winston's Folly." Several French officers, upon being presented with the idea of the tank, replied: "Wouldn't it be simpler to flood the Artois [River] and get your fleet there?"

The person Churchill had put in charge of the tank development program wrote to Churchill in frustration: "After losing the great advantage of your influence, I had considerable difficulty in steering the scheme past the rocks of opposition and the more insidious shoals of apathy, which are frequented by red herrings which cross the main life of progress at frequent intervals."

"Remember the elephants of Roman times," Churchill wrote in a letter. "These are mechanical elephants to break wire and earthwork phalanges." He urged that the tanks be held back from battle until they could be used in sufficient number to have a decisive effect. "Don't familiarize the enemy by degrees with these methods of attack," Churchill wrote in a memorandum about the place of the tank in a combined tactical offensive. "Apply them when all is ready on the largest possible scale, and with the priceless advantage of surprise." His advice was disregarded. Tanks were deployed for the first time in 1917 at the Battle of the Somme, but there were only 15 on the field. Though they proved a success in battle, the numbers were obviously too small to break the stalemate and carry the day. Churchill was greatly disappointed: "My poor 'land battleships' have been let off prematurely and on a petty scale," he wrote in a letter to a colleague. Many military men without Churchill's imagination thought the early battlefield trials of the tank were unimpressive, leading Churchill to complain that "gilded wiseacres were beginning to unearth again their original condemnations of such unprofessional expedients."

Tanks were used in greater numbers and to greater effect in the closing months of the war in 1918—thanks in large part to Churchill's subsequent efforts to boost tank production when he became minister of munitions in 1917. The new prime minister, David Lloyd-George, told the House of Commons in a debate in 1916 that "these suggestions [for the tank] would never have fructified had it not been for the fact that Mr. Churchill, who was then First Lord of the Admiralty, gave practical effect to them by making the necessary experiments, setting up committees for carrying the suggestions into effect, and by putting the whole of his energy and strength towards materializing the hopes of those who had been looking forward to an attempt of this kind." After the war, a special Royal Commission on War Inventions concluded that "it was primarily due to the receptivity, courage, and driving force" of Churchill that the idea of the tank "was converted into a practical shape."

The Appendix discusses a number of Churchill's other innovative ideas, such as labor arbitration boards, labor exchanges, and various social insurance programs. In nearly all cases, Churchill had to overcome resistance and bureaucratic obstacles. There are no secret strategies or silver-bullet solutions for cutting through resistance to change and innovation. In each case, Churchill used the full measure of his influence, authority, and persuasive power to promote innovations and changes. He sought highly skilled and forceful subordinates to execute his designs.

CHURCHILL ON INNOVATION

• *Innovation is as much a matter of willpower as imagination.* Churchill's maxim: "It is only possible to test the practicality of schemes . . . by pushing them vigorously forward in the teeth of obstacles, being quite sure these obstacles are not likely to give way easily to testing pressure."

CHAPTER 10

SUBSTANCE OVER STYLE

Moral Purpose, Destiny, and the Force of Personal Leadership

———————

A Government should keep its ear to the ground but they should also remember that this is not a very dignified attitude. . . . The British nation will find it very hard to look up to leaders who are detected in that somewhat ungainly posture.
> —WINSTON S. CHURCHILL, 1953

Rule shows the man.
> —ARISTOTLE

I N A N A G E where cigar smoking and scotch drinking are enjoying an astonishing comeback, Churchill will remain a popular and fascinating figure because of his large and colorful personality. Although no male executive in this day and age would dare dictate to a female secretary from his bathtub, the Churchillian practice of an afternoon nap is even gaining gradual acceptance in many executive suites. Churchill's grand style understandably inspires imitation.

I have tried to divide up and enumerate the various habits and aspects of Churchill's leadership style, though no mere listing of his attributes will be adequate to convey the sum of his leadership ability. Nor is leadership a matter of style alone. The genuine leader is in the end a person of substance. It is tempting to say that there is a missing X factor that completed Churchill's skills and provided him with the margin of judgment to go one way or another depending on the circumstances. For example, most of the time Churchill depended on personal persuasion to get his way, and he conducted most meetings as an honest broker and conciliator. He was a great believer—perhaps excessively so—in the ability of goodwill and personal contact to solve almost any problem. There were other times, however, when Churchill would put his foot down and impose his personal will in a highly forceful and even theatrical manner.

When Churchill went off to France to take a battalion command in the trenches in World War I, he knew that, as a disgraced politician, he might not get a warm welcome from the troops in the line. One of his subordinates described Churchill's first meal with the officers' mess:

> It was quite the most uncomfortable lunch I have ever been at. Churchill didn't say a word: he went right round the table staring each officer out of countenance. We had disliked the idea of Churchill being in command; now, having seen him, we disliked the idea even more. At the end of lunch, he made a short speech: "Gentlemen, I am now your Commanding Officer. Those who support me I will look after. Those who go against me I will break. Good afternoon gentlemen."

Nonetheless, Churchill quickly won over the affection and respect of his fellow officers and soldiers. Contrary to the initial impression that he would be a "tough guy," he gained a reputation for leniency and generosity with his troops. He forgave minor offenses that other commanders punished strictly. He was especially indulgent of infractions by troops who had seen hard fighting.

The most dramatic example of Churchill resorting to personal force and willfulness came when he had been prime minister for less than three weeks—on May 28, 1940. It is an episode that many of the biographies and heroic accounts of his leadership during Britain's "finest hour" pass over too quickly. However, it is possible to argue that this was the decisive trial of Churchill's life.

It is important to understand that, although Churchill's wartime leadership is universally acclaimed today, at the time he became prime minister in May 1940 many of his peers thought his tenure would be short-lived, and that the mantle of leadership would quickly pass to someone more sound. "This is *not* the last war administration by a long way," one leading member of Churchill's own party remarked. "Seldom can a Prime Minister have taken office,"

John Colville wrote in his diary, "with the Establishment . . . so dubious of the choice and so prepared to find its doubts justified." Churchill's own party failed to applaud him on his first visit to the House of Commons after becoming prime minister; it was left to the opposition Labour Party members to cheer their nation's new leader.

Even Churchill had his doubts about his position. While he was driving home from Buckingham Palace on May 10 after having received the King's appointment as prime minister, Churchill said to an aide: "I hope that it is not too late. I am very much afraid that it is. We can only do our best." It is hard to imagine a more difficult first two weeks in office. He had already been over to France twice in hope of staving off a complete collapse, but the situation continued to deteriorate rapidly. The British Expeditionary Force had been cut off and was facing destruction or capture on the beaches of France; it was not then apparent whether the Dunkirk evacuation would succeed in saving much of the army. After burning with ambition for high office all his life, he wrote to one of his predecessors at this time, "I'm not having very much fun being Prime Minister."

It was at this dire moment that Churchill faced a growing movement within his own small war cabinet to consider asking Italy (which at that point had not entered the war on the side of Germany) to mediate with Germany for peace terms. Lord Halifax, who was foreign minister in the cabinet and had been the alternative to Churchill for prime minister three weeks previously, pushed this idea vigorously. (It is possible that Halifax had already contacted Italian diplomats in London.) Churchill and others in the war cabinet thought such an appeal would be fatal to British and French morale. The chiefs of staff had just that day issued a report concluding that the key factor in Britain's ability to hold out would be morale. Nevertheless, Halifax was a powerful figure in the cabinet and in the Conservative Party, and he doubtless represented a substantial opinion within the party. Neville Chamberlain, whose position was still formidable, was beginning to warm to the idea. At a strained war cabinet meeting on May 27, Churchill and Halifax exchanged "heated words" over the matter. Halifax threatened to resign, which might bring down Churchill's premiership.

The following day—May 28—the argument was taken up again in the afternoon meeting of the war cabinet, while rumors of the breach were spreading quickly through senior government circles. Churchill argued that "nations which went down fighting rose again, but those which surrendered tamely were finished." Despite Churchill's strenuous arguments against peace negotiations, Halifax did not give ground. But the war cabinet meeting had to adjourn so that a scheduled meeting of the full cabinet—nearly 25 ministers in all—could convene at 6 P.M. Here would be Churchill's opportunity to isolate Halifax and put an end to the idea of peace negotiations.

"There now occurred one of the most extraordinary scenes of the war," Martin Gilbert wrote in his biography of Churchill. Tired after a long day of mostly bad news, Churchill opened the meeting with a survey of the war situation at that moment. The Dunkirk evacuation was under way with uncertain prospects for success; only a few troops had been evacuated so far. Meanwhile, he expected that Hitler would take Paris and "offer terms," after which he expected that the Italians would threaten war and also offer peace terms. There was no doubt, Churchill said, "that we must decline and fight on."

Hugh Dalton, the minister for economic warfare, recorded in paraphrase and direct quotation in his diary what Churchill said next:

And then he said, "I have thought carefully in these last days whether it was part of my duty to consider entering into negotiations with That Man." But it was idle to think that, if we tried to make peace now, we should get better terms than if we fought it out. The Germans would demand our fleet—that would be called "disarmament"—our naval bases, and much else. We should become a slave state, though a British Government which would be Hitler's puppet would be set up. . . .

"And I am convinced," he concluded, "that every man of you would rise up and tear me down from my place if I were for one moment to contemplate parley or surrender. If this long island story of ours is to end at last, let it end only when each one of us lies choking in his own blood upon the ground."

"Not much more was said," Dalton's diary entry continued. "No one expressed even the faintest flicker of dissent." Churchill's own recollection of the event in his war memoirs noted, "There then occurred a demonstration which, considering the character of the gathering—twenty-five experienced politicians and Parliament men, who represented all the different points of view, whether right or wrong, before the war—surprised me. Quite a number seemed to jump up from the table and come running to my chair, shouting and patting me on the back." When the smaller war cabinet met again at 7:30 P.M., the official minutes record that Churchill said "He did not remember having ever heard a gathering of persons occupying high places in political life express themselves so emphatically." Churchill had isolated Halifax and squashed the idea of peace negotiations once and for all. Neville Chamberlain swung round fully to Churchill's side, echoing his determination to fight on. Now not even Halifax's resignation could undermine Churchill's position. (As it was, Halifax fell in behind Churchill and became a loyal supporter. Just to be sure, however, Churchill later sent Halifax to Washington D.C. as ambassador, and replaced him as foreign secretary with Anthony Eden.) Hugh Dalton's diary entry added: "The man, and the only man we have, for this hour."

The point of this episode, though, is that from time to time, and especially in a crisis, the genuine leader must simply exert his personal force and summon up his *willfulness*. Churchill's demonstration of May 28 was dramatic and theatrical—what we would today call "over the top." But it also showed that Churchill's most famous lyric of resolve—"Never, never, never, never give in"—was not just a speech. In our consensual, cooperative age, asserting one's will in this way is considered bad form, but that may be one reason we have a dearth of genuine leaders.

But this is also the most delicate aspect of leadership, and why the arena where leadership is crucial above all others—military command—is always carefully bounded by hierarchy and structure. Nothing can so quickly ruin both morale and an organization itself than the willfulness of a leader who leads for the wrong objects.

We know that Churchill had read Machiavelli, and had given copies of Machiavelli's most famous book, *The Prince*, to several friends. Although direct references to Machiavelli by Churchill are rare, there are several instances in his words and career where distinct echoes of the great Florentine political philosopher occur. For example, while Churchill's normal mode was to deliberate and persuade in council with his colleagues and advisers, the episode of the peace negotiation issue recounted here shows that at times he would eschew further deliberation and simply decide a question once and for all on his own terms while steamrollering any dissent. One of Machiavelli's axioms in *The Prince* is that "one concludes that good counsel, from wherever it comes, must arise from the prudence of the prince, and not the prudence of the prince from good counsel." In other words, sometimes the rightness of an idea is determined not by collective deliberation, but by the simple force of the leader's willfulness. (Other Machiavellian echoes in Churchill are more precise. In *The Prince*, Machiavelli wrote that "a disorder should never be allowed to continue so as to avoid a war, because that is not to avoid it but to defer it to your disadvantage." In his passage attacking the infamous Munich agreement in *The Gathering Storm*, Churchill wrote: "There is no merit in putting off a war for a year if, when it comes, it is a far worse war or one much harder to win.")

But to suggest an affinity between Churchill and Machiavelli is to raise a grave problem, because Machiavelli's name has entered the language as an adjective—*Machiavellian*—suggesting amorality, if not immorality. There is little in the record of Hitler or Stalin, for example, that was not anticipated—and even encouraged—by Machiavelli. The only way to resolve this dilemma is to recognize that in evaluating a leader's skills, one must judge his actions with reference to the moral purpose toward which his actions are directed. Hitler also forcefully imposed his will on his colleagues on many occasions, but the difference between Hitler's willfulness and Churchill's can only be reckoned by reference to the ends they served. Health, intelligence, and shrewdness are all good things in the abstract, but they are bad things in a bad person. Health, intelligence, and shrewdness were bad things for Hitler, because they enabled him to serve evil ends. This is why questions of leadership are ultimately questions of *character*. In the end, leadership is not primarily a matter of intellect. John Keegan, author of several leading books on war strategy, has written of Churchill: "It is the moral rather than the intellectual content of his judgment that dominates."

Churchill himself explained this theme in a speech in Norway in 1948:

Human judgment may fail. You may act very wisely, you think, but it may turn out a great failure. On the other hand, one may do a foolish thing which may turn out well. I have seen many things happen, but the fact remains that human life is presented to us as a simple choice between right and wrong. If you obey that law you will find that that way is far safer in the long run than all calculation which can ever be made. I want to say this to you because that is something my experience has taught me. But I certainly do not want you to understand me to say that

I have always done the right thing—I should be ashamed to claim that. But I do have the feeling that one must act in accordance with what one feels and believes.

While it may not be possible to learn and assimilate the intuitive genius for strategy that Churchill enjoyed, it is certainly possible to understand some of the basic aspects of good character that were central to his leadership. Again the contrast with Hitler is instructive. Though as we have seen Churchill was capable of asserting his willfulness in the most forceful way, as in the "choking in our own blood" speech, he drew the line at a different point than the one Hitler chose. Hitler frequently overruled his generals; Churchill never did. Though he would often argue strenuously with his chiefs of staff, as mentioned in Chapter 6, Churchill did not overrule their decisions or reject their counsel. ("He had learned his lesson in a hard school," one of his aides observed, referring to the Dardanelles experience.) Hitler executed some of his military commanders who defied him; Churchill preferred advisers who would argue a case confidently against him.

The key ingredient to Churchill's character emerges by contrast with his great adversary Hitler: magnanimity. Churchill's largeness of soul not only comprised his deep attachment to moral purpose, but also his kindness, regard, and sense of fair play toward his colleagues, subordinates, and fellow citizens. It explains the moral he attached to his books on World War II: "In War: Resolution; In Defeat: Defiance; In Victory: Magnanimity; In Peace, Goodwill." It explains why he said that "I have always been against the Pacifists during the quarrel, and against the Jingoes at the close." It explains why, during a summit meeting with Stalin and FDR where Stalin suggested that following Germany's defeat 100,000 Germans should be gathered up and summarily executed (FDR countered with 50,000), an indignant Churchill rose from the dinner table and stormed out of the room. It explains the famous story of a teary-eyed Churchill surveying the heavy bomb damage in London during the blitz in 1940; a woman picking up the ruins of her demolished home, cheered by Churchill's arrival, said to a companion, "See, he really cares."

From his earliest days Churchill was absorbed with a moral vision for his life. "Civilization," he wrote in 1900, is "the state of society where moral forces begin to escape from the tyranny of physical forces." "Ladies and gentlemen," he said in his first political speech, "I stand for Liberty!" In 1899 he forecast that "The new century will witness the great war for the existence of the Individual." He rejected socialism and Communism because, he said, they were based on the social morality of the anthill. His abiding faith in the goodness of democracy and individual liberty was also the bedrock of his candor and adherence to telling the truth.

It is the rightness of moral vision combined with the qualities of character that provide us with confidence in the possibility of leadership, and the means for understanding the bounds of a leader's sheer willfulness that is necessary from time to time. The lesson of a leader's measured willfulness is perhaps best epitomized by the old-fashioned Western movie, where the occasionally brutal autocracy of the town sheriff is necessary to maintain a just order in a frontier town that might easily degrade to anarchy and barbarism. But because of the moral magnitude of these situations, the town sheriff was always presented as an unimpeachable character portrayed by Gary Cooper or Henry Fonda or John Wayne. It is no accident that Churchill was a great fan of American Westerns, and they may have bolstered his belief that "Moral force is, unhappily, no substitute for armed force, but it is a very great reinforcement."

Just as human law is not self-enforcing, so too human organizations are not self-executing structures that run all by themselves. They must be driven forward relentlessly. A leader's calculations about a particular decision may be wrong, but the trustworthiness of a leader's character offers a sufficient counterweight on the balance sheet. It was precisely Churchill's forcefulness and resolve on issues throughout his career, about which many British citizens thought he had been wrong, that served as a source of reassurance when Britain stood alone in 1940.

There is a final aspect of the X factor that illuminates Churchill's leadership ability that is even less susceptible to precise analysis than character. This is the aspect of *destiny*. Churchill wrote and spoke of his sense of destiny often, from his youth to his last years. One of his most famous passages appears in the last paragraph of *The Gathering Storm* (the first of six volumes on World War II), describing his sentiments upon having become prime minister at last: "I was conscious of a profound sense of relief. At last I had the authority to give directions over the whole scene. I felt as if I were walking with destiny, and that all my past life had been but a preparation for this hour and for this trial." Long before, shortly after escaping from a prisoner of war camp in South Africa during the Boer War and making his way through enemy territory back to British-held land, he had reflected:

> I found no comfort in any of the philosophical ideas which
> some men parade in their hours of ease and strength and safety.
> They seemed only fair weather friends. I realized with awful
> force that no exercise of my own feeble wit and strength could
> save me from my enemies, and that without the assistance of
> that High Power which interferes in the eternal sequence of
> causes and effects more often than we are always prone to ad-
> mit, I could never succeed.

Churchill used to attribute his several near misses and narrow escapes from death in the trenches of World War I to the hand of destiny; though his political fortunes were at low ebb at that time, he wrote to his wife, "My conviction that the greatest of my work is still to be done is strong within me and I ride reposefully along the gale." He also used to recall a maxim written by his ancestor

Marlborough: "As I think most things are settled by destiny, when one has done one's best, the only thing is to await the result with patience." After he lost a close election in 1950, after which most observers thought his political career was certain to be over, he remarked to a secretary "I know I am going to be Prime Minister again. I know it." (He took up that office for the last time the following year.)

A sense of destiny is often a strong feature of the inner life of great leaders. There is an almost mystical quality to the sense of destiny that was a part of the conscious life of Napoleon, Lincoln, Theodore Roosevelt, and Churchill. There are elements of romance along with destiny in the Churchill story. Few people are given the chance to, in effect, live their lives over again. In some ways World War II was Churchill's chance to do just that. He began World War II as he had begun World War I, as First Lord of the Admiralty. He was facing the same foe, and that foe was invading France along the very same routes it had traced in 1914. His Norway initiative miscarried in some of the same ways as the Dardanelles campaign, after almost the same amount of elapsed time as in World War I. But this time the rest of the story would be different.

Ironically, Churchill's sense of his own destiny had actually deserted him on the eve of his moment of destiny. In 1937 Churchill had reflected on the idea of living one's life over again in an essay called "A Second Choice." The eminent political philosopher Harry Jaffa observed that this essay might well have been called "A Second Chance." Churchill began,

> If I had to live my life over again in the same surroundings, no
> doubt I should have the same perplexities and hesitations;
> no doubt I should have my same sense of proportion, my
> same guiding lights, my same onward thrust, my same limita-
> tions. And if these came into contact with the same external
> facts, would I not run in fact along exactly the same grooves?
> Of course if the externals are varied, if accident and chance

flow out through new uncharted channels, I shall vary accordingly. But then I should not be living my life over again. I should be living another life in a world whose structure and history would to a large extent diverge from this one.

At the time Churchill wrote this, he was out of office, over 60 years old, and thinking that his career was all but over. "Modern conditions," he also wrote at that time, "do not lend themselves to the production of the heroic or superdominant type." In other words, Churchill did not think that his like would ever be seen on the world stage again. Moreover, Churchill wrote, "I do not seek to tread again the toilsome and dangerous path. Not even an opportunity of making a different set of mistakes and experiencing a different series of adventures would lure me."

The fact that Churchill was mistaken about his own prospects and the role he was shortly to play on the world stage does not cast a cloud over either his judgment or the idea of personal destiny. Quite the opposite: It provides us with confidence, however inchoate and undefinable, that destiny does play a genuine role in summoning leadership when it is needed. The corollary is that leaders or would-be leaders should always be ready. Destiny may not thrust supreme trials in our path, but the virtues and habits of mind necessary for a supreme trial will prove just as useful in less supreme matters of business and everyday life. Had World War II not thrust the supreme trial on Churchill, he would today be a subject of minor historical interest, like many of his contemporaries. But his virtues and habits of mind would still be well worth study and emulation, for even without the war, it would still be true that he was the kind of man about whom it was rightly said that "nobody left his presence without feeling a braver man."

A BIOGRAPHICAL SKETCH OF CHURCHILL'S EXECUTIVE CAREER

CHURCHILL'S EARLY RISE to prominence in British politics owed partly to his being born to an illustrious family, but his family was also a problem for him. His father, Lord Randolph Churchill, had led a long and distinguished political career culminating in his appointment as chancellor of the exchequer in 1886, when Winston was 11. Randolph's career suffered a fatal blow when he resigned from the cabinet shortly after, however, and within a decade Randolph had died following a long degenerative illness (said to be syphilis) that robbed him of his sanity. The Churchill family name was in some disgrace at the time Winston began contemplating a political career.

Churchill's own reputation began to rise following the early successes of his wartime journalism, beginning with a book on his adventures in India (*The Story of the Malakand Field Force*) and with Lord Kitchener's army in the Sudan (*The River War*). Following a loss at his first try for Parliament, he set off again as a war correspondent in South Africa during the Boer War. Captured by the Boers, Churchill escaped from prisoner of war camp and made his way back through enemy territory. The sensational tale of his capture and escape made him a nationally celebrated figure in England, and quickly propelled him into Parliament in 1900. His early speeches in Parliament were noteworthy, and within five years he had received his first ministerial appointment—at age 31.

For an American reader to fully appreciate the nature of Churchill's executive posts, it is helpful to consider how British government works, and the relation of ministers to the prime minister, the cabinet, and the House of Commons. The constitutional features of the British parliamentary system differ markedly from the American constitutional scheme, which emphasizes clear executive authority and the separation of powers. Unlike American government, where the president is elected separately from the legislative branch and names whomever he wants to serve in his cabinet, the prime minister and the other ministers of the British cabinet are typically chosen from among members of the House of Commons, and the House of Commons oversees their executive authority closely. The British cabinet is much larger than its American counterpart—as many as 40 members. While they derive their ultimate mandate from the voters just as in any democracy, the prime minister and the individual ministers depend for their day-to-day tenure on the support of a majority in the House of Commons. Even though the prime minister names the cabinet, the cabinet's relation to the House of Commons allows individual ministers to have their own base of support, making them relatively more independent of the prime minister than American departmental heads are of the president. A minister with a strong personal following in the House has more latitude to chart his own course with his department. While American cabinet secretaries serve wholly at the pleasure of the president and can be removed by the president at any time, a prime minister cannot easily remove a cabinet minister unless the prime minister is confident of commanding support in the House. Conversely, the resignation of a key minister can threaten the entire government or bring down a prime minister, if the House of Commons votes a no-confidence motion.

What this all means is that the prime minister is in many ways weaker than the president of the United States. As the title prime minister implies, he or she is first among equals, and his or her preeminence depends upon personal force of leadership much more than does that of the American president. Because of this constitutional circumstance, the British cabinet is regarded as a collectively responsible body, and it acts somewhat as a mini deliberative body, meeting frequently to discuss the wide range of policies from all government departments. The British cabinet and its ministers are intended chiefly to set out the broad outlines of policy, and leave the actual administration to the permanent civil service in each department. The American cabinet, by contrast, meets irregularly (and does not really need to meet at all), seldom advises the president collectively about policy, and cabinet secretaries are intended to be hands-on executive administrators at their individual departments. (Another crucial difference to keep in mind as this analysis proceeds is that unlike the American president, who is explicitly designated in the Constitution to be the commander in chief of the military, the British prime minister is not designated as the commander in chief of the military. Civilian control of the military in Britain is less clear-cut than in the United States.) A prime minister does not enjoy the same latitude to overrule a cabinet secretary as an American president does. A prime minister will overrule a cabinet minister with reluctance, and usually only with the strong support of most of the other cabinet ministers. This diffusion of power across the group may explain the difference in terminology: an American always speaks of the government as a singular "it" while "the government" in British terminology is understood to be plural.

Churchill's style was a major departure from the typical manner of a cabinet minister, and it was this exceptional "contempt for the conventional" and "engaging plain-spokenness" (as his friend Wilfred Blunt put it) that led to much of the criticism against him. In many respects, Churchill's style was more suited for an American administration than for the British cabinet. From his first appointment, both friends and critics remarked on his remarkable energy, his quick mind and imagination, and his tendency to cast his attention far afield beyond his own ministerial portfolio. It is easy to see how his energy

and audacity could be regarded as presumption, and how his eagerness could offend his colleagues. Beginning with his very first administrative post, "Churchill made it his business," his son Randolph
wrote, "to acquaint himself with many aspects of government and
to express his views on them. . . . While he was a backbencher,
Churchill had spoken as if he were an Under-Secretary, now, as an
Under-Secretary, as if a member of the Cabinet; and when he reached
the Cabinet he was apt to speak as if he were Prime Minister."

Beginning with his very first administrative post in 1905, as
under-secretary of state for the colonies, it is possible to discern
several hallmarks of Churchill's executive style, especially his constant readiness to exploit opportunities and seek great responsibility
and authority. Churchill had originally been offered an under-secre-
taryship at the Treasury Office. He turned down this more presti-
gious appointment in favor of the Colonial Office for a savvy reason:
the cabinet secretary he would serve under was Lord Elgin, and
under the British system, a member of the House of Lords may not
appear in the House of Commons. This meant that Churchill would
get to manage the Colonial Office's business before the House,
which was nearly as good as being a full member of the cabinet. (As
viewers of *Question Time* on C-SPAN will know, members of the
House of Commons enjoy the right to put pointed questions about
policy to members of the cabinet.) Moreover, as Randolph Churchill
explained in his biography of his father, "since Elgin liked to spend
as much time as possible in Scotland he [Churchill] would be to a
large extent put in charge of his important department. . . . For an
Under-Secretary Churchill had exceptional opportunities."

Churchill made the most of the opportunity. Prior to this appointment, Churchill had no administrative experience. The circumstances of this post enabled him to gain a lot of experience in a
hurry, and he assumed the major responsibility for the entire work of
the Colonial Office. Indeed, Churchill's eagerness to assume as
much authority as possible relieved Lord Elgin from having to exercise close oversight. Lord Elgin wrote to Churchill in 1907: "I am

glad to say that with the exception of our two spoilt children, New-foundland & Natal, I have not much to say of Office matters."

Churchill had taken this post shortly after the end of the Boer War in South Africa. With the fighting concluded, territorial settlements and adjustments were required. Churchill oversaw the delicate and complicated deliberations for a creation of self-government in the Transvaal, where previously warring factions of Dutch and British settlers must now find a means to get along. Parliamentary opinion was divided about the balance of interests that would exist under alternative drafts of a Transvaal constitution, and Churchill was at the vortex of the criticism and concern over the issue. Churchill held a steady bearing throughout, defending a compromise constitution against its critics from many sides, and conceding minor adjustments in the face of majority sentiment. Reflecting on the episode in a letter to the King, Churchill wrote:

> All S. African business in the House of Commons has been left entirely in my hands. I have had to speak more than any other minister except Mr. Birrell & to answer something like 500 questions, besides a great number of supplementary questions put & answered on the spur of the moment. I have had no previous experience in this kind of work. I have had a new & unfathomed House of Commons to deal with in respect of subjects upon which it is strangely excited; & at least four perfectly separate currents of opinion to consider.

This passage is vintage Churchill, displaying both his tenacity at tackling a controversial problem and his ability to refine and comprehend the main points at issue in an orderly fashion. To Prime Minister Asquith, who had proposed moving Churchill to the Local Government Office in March 1908, Churchill wrote: "I *know* the Colonial Office. It is a post of immense, but largely unconnected, detail; & I have special experience of several kinds which helps. . . . During the past two years practically all the constructive action & all the Parliamentary exposition has been mine. I have many threads in hand and many plans in movement." A new under-secretary, Churchill argued, could not hope to master the office during the time left to the present government before the next election.

Although his restless energy and wide-ranging initiative caused some friction with his superior, Lord Elgin, Churchill also expressed gratitude for the opportunity he had enjoyed. After a year and half in the post, Churchill wrote to Lord Elgin: "No one could ever have had a more trustful & indulgent chief than I have been most lucky to find on first joining a Government; & I have learned a very great deal in the conduct of official business from your instruction and example which I should all my life have remained completely ignorant of, if I had gone elsewhere." When Churchill was leaving the Colonial Office in 1908 to take up his first cabinet-level post as President of the Board of Trade, Lord Elgin paid tribute to Churchill, writing to a friend, Lord Crewe:

> When I accepted Churchill as my Under-Secretary I knew I had no easy task. I resolved to give him access to all business— but to keep control (& my temper). I think I may say I succeeded. Certainly we have had no quarrel during the last $2\frac{1}{2}$ years, on the contrary he has again and again thanked me for what he had learned and for our pleasant personal relations. I have taken a keen interest in his ability and in many ways attractive personality.

When he arrived at the Board of Trade (which at that time was roughly equivalent to the U.S. Department of Commerce and Department of Labor), Churchill, according to his son Randolph, is reported to have said "there is nothing to do here." But, in typical Churchillian fashion, "he took a more extensive view of the purpose of his department than had his predecessors," and made the Board of Trade the instrument for advancing a number of broad social policy initiatives that had been taking shape in his mind for some time. Paul Addison provides a helpful observation of how Churchill came to regard the work of the Board of Trade: "The functions of the Board of Trade in employment policy resembled those of the Intelligence Department in the Army, which did not govern policy or command troops, but studied war, accumulated and sifted information, and prepared plans."

Churchill had been pondering for a long time various social insurance schemes "to spread a net over the abyss" of poverty. While still at the Colonial Office Churchill had written to Prime Minister Herbert Asquith about his broad design. "Dimly across gulfs of ignorance I see the outline of a policy which I call the Minimum Standard. It is national rather than departmental." The "Minimum Standard" was Churchill's contribution to the origin of the British welfare state, which Churchill at other times referred to as "the meshes of our safety net"—another of his phrases that has entered our common vocabulary. While the British welfare state, like every other modern welfare state, grew out of hand and now requires significant pruning, it is important to recall Churchill's balanced view of the objectives of social policy. These were the years when Churchill was known as a radical. To be sure, Churchill had been influenced deeply by early sociological literature about the degradation of poverty in England's cities, especially Seebohm Rowntree's *Poverty: A Study in Town Life*, and J. A. Hobson's *Problems of Poverty*. In a review of Rowntree's book in 1901, Churchill wrote:

> Consider the peculiar case of these poor, and the consequences. Although the British Empire is so large, they cannot find room to live in it; although it is so magnificent, they would have had a better chance of happiness, if they had been born cannibal islanders of the Southern seas; although its science is so profound, they would have been more healthy if they had been subjects of Hardicanute.

But Churchill was no redistributionist or socialist. As with so many of his other objectives throughout his long career, he sought a middle course between the extremes, adjusting his positions depending on changing circumstances. Again, it is crucial to understand what Churchill held to be "the larger object in view" at the time. During this phase of his political life, Churchill was worried about the rising enthusiasm for socialism, especially its revolutionary variant that would break over the world ferociously in just a few years. Some of this dangerous revolutionary fervor could be detected in the newly rising Labour Party. Although Randolph Churchill allowed in his biography of Winston that "Churchill had flirted with the idea of collectivism as a means of solving social problems," by the time he was advocating the policies making up the "Minimum Standard" at the Board of Trade and later at the Home Office, Churchill had worked out his "center position," drawing a distinction between Socialism and his own brand of Liberalism. This "center position" became a dominant theme of Churchill's speeches in 1908, at a time when he was otherwise engaged in a political struggle against the prerogatives of the House of Lords—a cause that would give much aid and comfort to radical and egalitarian sensibilities. In a speech in 1908 Churchill laid out the distinction:

> Socialism wants to pull down wealth, Liberalism seeks to raise up poverty. Socialism would destroy private interests—Liberalism would preserve them in the only way they could justly be preserved, by reconciling them with public right. Socialism seeks to kill enterprise. Liberalism seeks to rescue enterprise from the trammels of privilege and preference. Socialism assails the maximum pre-eminence of the individual—Liberalism seeks to build up the minimum standard of the masses. Socialism attacks capital, Liberalism attacks monopoly.

"An extreme Socialist policy would plunge the country into a violent social struggle," he had said in a speech in January, "and there would be no pensions for anybody at all. No, the future lies with us. We tread the middle path between the party of reaction on the one side and the party of revolution on the other." And in a speech in March 1908, Churchill made an argument about economic central planning that would anticipate the critique of economic calculation under socialism and the "knowledge problem" made more fully by Ludwig von Mises and F. A. Hayek two decades later:

> I distrust profoundly the positive intervention of Government—particularly party Government—in the delicate and intricate world-wide operations of trade. They do not understand it. I reject as impracticable the insane Socialist idea that we could have a system whereby the whole national production of the country, with all its infinite ramifications, should be organized and directed by a permanent official, however able, from some central office. The idea is not only impossible, but unthinkable. If it was even attempted it would produce a most terrible shrinkage and destruction of productive energy.
> I am drawn to the conclusion that the intervention of Government in regard to trade must be mainly of a liberating character, of a negative character in that sense.

Later in his career, especially after World War II, Churchill would become a vocal champion of property rights and private enterprise against the onslaught of Labour Party drives to extend socialism. But at this point in his career Churchill was very much a Progressive. He was an admirer of Progressive reform in the United States. There were, he thought, specific and limited initiatives consonant with the purposes of different government departments that could be undertaken to help promote the economic progress of the nation.

One of the mandates of the Board of Trade was to mediate industrial disputes, a duty Churchill relished. The Board of Trade was enabled by law to appoint conciliators for industrial disputes. Churchill often stepped into a dispute as mediator rather than appoint someone else. In his first year as its president, the Board of Trade mediated more conciliation cases than in the previous two years combined. This post first offered Churchill an arena for his formidable negotiating skills.

With his penchant for organizational and systematic refinement, Churchill proposed to improve the conciliation process by creating a

Standing Court of Arbitration. This five-member court would comprise two labor representatives, two management representatives, and a chairman named by the Board of Trade. (The chairmen of these courts, Churchill was quick to say, must be "persons of eminence and impartiality.") With this administrative innovation, Churchill thought, the government would be able to intervene earlier in industrial disputes. Moreover, he thought that a mechanism that explicitly recognized the interests of labor in the membership of the court "will remove from the Court the reproach which workmen have sometimes brought against individual Conciliators and Arbitrators, that, however fair they may be, they do not intimately understand the position of the manual laborer . . . the decisions of the Court would be rendered more authoritative." Churchill's new courts came into operation in the fall of 1908, and in the following 12 months this new mechanism was used successfully to resolve disputes in the boot and shoe, coal mining, and iron and copper industries.

Churchill's second large initiative at the Board of Trade was the development of a broad new policy to combat unemployment. As the Board of Trade was charged with overseeing the workings of the labor market, Churchill was concerned with finding a remedy for the problem of rising joblessness. Churchill had switched from the Conservative to the Liberal Party a few years before in large part over the issue of trade protectionism, which was the Conservatives' favored answer for the problem of unemployment. As a staunch opponent of protectionism, Churchill could not embrace this idea. At the same time, he could not embrace the socialist-inspired Labour Party demand for a right-to-a-job policy. Churchill and his colleagues in the cabinet and at the Board of Trade decided to move forward with a scheme that would combine unemployment insurance with a system of "labor exchanges," by which employers would notify unemployed workers of job vacancies. (This was in the days before classified ads in the newspapers.) Churchill thought that the failure to make more efficient use of an increasingly mobile labor force "clearly involves economic waste." But he also thought that a labor exchange was an essential cornerstone of unemployment insurance:

> The establishment of Labor Exchanges is necessary for the efficient working of the insurance scheme; for all foreign experiments have shown that a fund for insurance against unemployment needs to be protected against unnecessary or fraudulent claims by the power of notifying situations to men in receipt of benefit so soon as any situations become vacant. The insurance scheme, on the other hand, will be a lever of the most valuable kind to bring the Exchanges into successful operation. . . . The administration of the twin measures must become increasingly interwoven.

Two aspects of the unfolding of this policy display classic Churchillian leadership style. First, contrary to the enduring criticism that Churchill rushed headlong with new ideas that had not been properly thought through, Churchill moved slowly and deliberately with the development of the labor exchange proposal. Over a period of months Churchill actively sought the advice of senior civil servants and outside observers (Sidney Webb, the leader of the Fabian socialist movement, was among them), and circulated to the cabinet a number of memoranda written chiefly by his staff.

Second, Churchill deployed his formidable negotiating and persuasive skills, along with a dash of cleverness, to sell the idea to employers and laborers, both of whom were skeptical. In the highly class-conscious worldview of the time, both management and labor feared the labor exchanges might tip the balance in favor of the other interest. The labor unions feared that the exchanges would enable employers to employ more nonunion labor, and even break strikes with nonunion workers. Employers feared that the exchanges would become hotbeds of union activity, and help increase union pressure on employers. Churchill played directly to this anxiety by arguing to both sides that each would gain the advantage, while agreeing to seek modifications to redress their greatest worries. To the Trades Union Congress (TUC), Churchill argued that the labor exchanges should be thought of as a potential recruiting apparatus. He agreed to a union demand that no worker would be prejudiced by refusing to take a job below the prevailing wage. On the other hand, Churchill refused to prevent labor exchanges from referring workers to employers involved in a labor dispute. To employers, Churchill offered assurances that unions could not use the labor exchanges to bring pressure on unorganized workers, because strict discipline would be maintained. Moreover, Churchill argued, "if anybody had said a year ago that the trade unions would have agreed to a government labor exchange sending 500 or 1,000 men to an employer whose men were out on strike . . . [nobody] would have believed it at all."

This might seem like two-faced dealing, but Churchill sincerely believed in the capacity of the government to be an honest broker among interests. It is true that at about this time, Churchill had been recommending Machiavelli's *The Prince* to several close friends. (Although Churchill sent copies of *The Prince* to Max Aitken and Lord John Fisher at about this time, no record survives regarding Churchill's detailed thoughts about Machiavelli.) But it is possible to discern the larger purpose Churchill had in mind, and to see his actions as means proportional to the ends. Citizens are rightly cynical about politicians who simply say what the group in front of them would like to hear, and the base flattery that has become so pervasive among politicians in our time has blinded us to those cases in which a genuine leader can partially embrace the prejudices of a group in order to serve some larger purpose. Abraham Lincoln's Temperance Address, which he delivered to a leading temperance group in 1842, is the highest model of exactly this kind of leadership, and is worthy of close study. At the time of this speech, the temperance movement was growing in strength and seemed destined to become a major force in American politics. But temperance was what we would call today a single-issue movement. Although Lincoln did not agree with the temperance policy of complete prohibition, like most people he could agree with the more noble and moderate aspects of temperance. No one is *for* drunkenness. In his Temperance Address, Lincoln sought to have the temperance movement connect its more noble purposes to a larger cause, and to understand themselves in a larger context. Lincoln could see, nearly 20 years before he became president, that the temperance vote would be a valuable and necessary component of a majority coalition to end slavery and uphold constitutional government, because the cause of abolition and the cause of reasonable temperance rested upon similar ground. A man cannot be free if he is held in the legal bondage of slavery, and neither can he be free if he is enslaved by alcohol. The great Lincoln scholar Harry V. Jaffa summarizes the design and effect of Lincoln's speech:

> The Temperance Address shows, as do few documents of modern politics, a method whereby a public man can both accept and reject the prejudices of his contemporaries; how he can, at one and the same time, flatter their vanity and chasten their egotism; how he can, appearing to agree with their opinions, modify them, however little, or failing that, so to promote his own leadership that, when these opinions come to be applied, they will be applied by a man whose judgment is not chained to them and who can thus utilize them for wiser purposes.

This is a perfect description of Churchill's motives and actions in his negotiations with each side of controversy over the new labor exchanges. This same shrewdness in service of a broader purpose shows up at many points in his career.

The last major initiative of Churchill's tenure at the Board of Trade was similar to the others: minimum wage and working condition legislation for what was known as the *sweated trades*—what we refer to today as sweatshops. The Trade Boards Act that emerged from this effort covered four trades—ready-made tailoring, paper box making, machine lace making, and chain making—in which nearly three-quarters of the 200,000 workers covered by the act were women. Again, even though Churchill was known during this period as a radical, he drew a distinction between these ameliorative measures and the full-throated socialism that more genuine radicals were urging:

> These methods of regulating wages by law are only defensible as exceptional measures to deal with diseased or parasitic trades. A gulf must be fixed between trades subject to such control and ordinary economic industry. A clear definition of sweated trades must comprise (a) wages *exceptionally* low, and (b) conditions prejudicial to physical and social welfare.

In a similar vein, Churchill also proposed to deal with cyclical unemployment through a variety of government stimuli, ranging from accelerating warship production to establishing new public works projects such as reforestation:

> There ought to be in permanent existence certain recognized industries of a useful, but uncompetitive character, like, we shall say, afforestation, managed by public departments, and capable of being expanded or contracted according to the needs of the labor market, just as easily as you can pull out the stops or work the pedals of an organ.

In addition, Churchill thought a "Committee of National Organization" should be formed analogous to the Committee of Imperial Defense that oversaw Britain's strategic affairs. Neither of these ideas came to pass, and Churchill abandoned this view later in his career as chancellor of the exchequer, when the Labour Party called for massive public works as a means to combat unemployment at the outset of the Great Depression.

After nearly two years as president of the Board of Trade, Churchill was ready for promotion. His tenure at the Board of Trade, though not universally acclaimed (nothing Churchill ever did achieved universal acclaim), was generally regarded as having been successful. Lord John Morley wrote to Churchill in January 1910, "Your position has now risen to the first order. Those are the moments that most demand circumspection." Churchill declined the

Irish Office because it was "an office of the second rank," though ironically Churchill would be deeply involved in the Irish controversy over the next 15 years. He would have liked an appointment as First Lord of the Admiralty (equivalent to our secretary of the Navy), because, as he wrote to Lord Morley, he had come to "realize what a tremendous part these warlike matters played in the inner life of a Liberal Cabinet." But the Admiralty post was occupied by Reginald McKenna, who was not interested in moving on to a new post. So in February Prime Minister Asquith elevated Churchill to home secretary, one of the premier cabinet posts. Churchill was 35, the second-youngest home secretary ever.

The Home Office is responsible for law and order, and supervises the police services, prisons, and many other aspects of criminal justice and public safety (including the fire departments). The Home Office unifies functions that in American government are separated among different agencies. The home secretary reviews all death sentences, and makes recommendations to the king for clemency or commutation. It is a wide-ranging office, requiring versatility in its chief. Paul Addison comments that "Almost every week Churchill had to juggle with a diversity of departmental problems."

At the Home Office Churchill continued the reform theme he had embraced at the Board of Trade. He embarked on an ambitious program of prison and sentencing reforms. Prison reform had already been an active policy under Churchill's predecessors, who had established a Prisons Commission as far back as 1877. Paul Addison comments, "A less imaginative politician than Churchill might well have concluded that penal reform had run its course, and a period of consolidation was needed. . . . Churchill, however, decided that much more needed to be done." His program included better prison conditions, educational programs for inmates, and the exclusion from prison of petty offenders and debtors. Churchill made it his rule to review the entire case record of every death sentence that came before him, much as an appellate judge might do. Again his organizational bent came to the fore in his thoughts on sentencing reform. He proposed that a Home Office Board of Classification be established to "consider the case of all offenders after their being sentenced, and distribute them to receive their appropriate treatment throughout the different penal corrective and curative institutions of the prison system."

Though Churchill strongly supported the death penalty, he recommended clemency at a higher rate than his predecessors. In his two years at the Home Office, he recommended it in 21 out of the 43 cases that came before him. Churchill also took the lead in Parliament in passing the Shops Act, which, like his Board of Trade initiatives aimed at working conditions in the sweated trades, set out maximum working hours for retail employees.

Churchill's social reform initiatives at the Home Office were overshadowed by several controversies involving labor strikes. At this early moment in the labor movement, strikes often became violent, and as the minister responsible for public safety, Churchill had to make difficult decisions about the use of force to restrain violent strikers. In the United States, it is customary to call out state-based National Guard units to assist local police in stopping riots, but this is not a decision made at the federal level. In Britain, there is no equivalent to the state-level National Guard; in the event that local unrest is greater than the capacity of the regular local police (who were then, as now, not well-armed for serious disturbances), the home secretary had to consider whether to dispatch the Metropolitan Police from London, or even call for the assistance of the army. On more than one occasion Churchill responded to outbreaks of union violence by ordering army troops to be placed in readiness to act, though he always sought a conciliatory and moderate course, ordering that maximum restraint should be used. Nevertheless, controversy over these episodes—especially over the unrest in the Welsh coal mining region around Tonypandy—would dog Churchill for years after. Union leaders blamed Churchill for a handful of deaths that occurred when strikers confronted army troops, while conservatives criticized Churchill for not intervening more forcefully. Most historians and biographers today laud Churchill's conduct in these episodes. For example, Norman Rose, Churchill's most recent biographer, notes that "The myth of Tonypandy—that, in November 1910, he had ordered the military to fire upon the striking miners of the Rhondda Valley—has no substance in fact. But the legend died hard, disproved but not dispelled. In fact, Churchill acted with admirable restraint in an explosive situation."

These incidents were to efface Churchill's reputation as a social reformer, and create permanent enmity between him and the labor unions, with whom he had hitherto enjoyed good relations. A Labour Party Member of Parliament had said that Churchill had brought "courage and a certain quality of imagination to the task of dealing with labour questions." Churchill had always been supportive of labor unions, remarking in Parliament several months after Tonypandy:

> I consider that every workman is well advised to join a trade union. I cannot conceive how any man standing undefended against the powers that be in this world could be so foolish, if he can possible spare the money from the maintenance of his family, not to associate himself with an organization to protect the rights and interests of labour.

It was about this same time, however, that unfolding world events began to change Churchill's thinking in profound ways and with large consequences for his future career. Up to this point Churchill had been chiefly concerned with social reform, and had not had much interest in military and foreign affairs, despite his military education and overseas experience. One of his first acts upon entering Parliament in 1900 was a ferocious opposition to a proposal to expand Britain's army. Randolph Churchill wrote in his biography of his father that "On foreign policy he took the same wrong-headed position as other Radicals on the Left and in the Liberal Party." In 1908 Churchill dismissed the idea that a European war might be in prospect: "I think it is greatly to be deprecated that persons should try to spread the belief in this country that war between Great Britain and Germany is inevitable. It is all nonsense." In 1909, Churchill opposed Admiralty proposals to expand naval shipbuilding, even though rapid German naval expansion was known to be under way. "I was still a skeptic about the danger of the European situation," Churchill wrote later in *The World Crisis*, "and not convinced by the Admiralty case."

But on the morning of July 1, 1911, Germany announced that it had dispatched the gunboat *Panther* to the French Moroccan port of Agadir to protect German interests. Germany and France were disputing territorial claims at the time, but the dispatch of the *Panther* indicated that Germany was prepared to contemplate action beyond diplomacy. Europe now entered a tense period, poised on the brink of general war. "All the alarm bells throughout Europe began immediately to quiver," Churchill wrote in *The World Crisis*. "I could not think of anything else but the peril of war. I did my other work as it came along, but there was only one field of interest fiercely illuminated in my mind. . . . Liberal politics, the People's Budget, Free Trade, Peace, Retrenchment and Reform—all the war cries of our election struggles began to seem unreal in the presence of this new pre-occupation."

The Agadir Crisis was resolved many weeks later through diplomacy, in which the credibility of the British threat to come to the aid of France in the event of war was probably the key factor. But it was a harbinger of events to come. In the midst of the Agadir Crisis, Churchill attended a day-long cabinet meeting in which prospective military strategy was discussed. From this meeting it became clear that Britain was unprepared for a serious war, and moreover that its vaunted navy was not properly organized for modern warfare. There were profound differences of view between the army and the navy concerning war strategy and how each service was to work with the other. The navy lacked a war planning staff similar to the General Staff that had long guided the army. Following the end of the meeting, Secretary of State for War Richard Haldane told Prime

Minister Asquith that he would not continue at the War Office unless there were reforms in the navy, most especially the creation of a proper Naval War Staff. Senior naval officers strongly resisted this idea. "The navy of that day," military historian Richard Ollard has observed, "was hostile to criticism, suspicious of change and development, except for minor improvements within well-established enclaves, and prejudiced against intellectuals and general ideas." The current First Lord of the Admiralty, Reginald McKenna, refused to overrule the naval establishment about this matter, so Asquith resolved to make a change at the Admiralty. In October 1911, Asquith asked Churchill to become First Lord of the Admiralty.

Churchill served at the Admiralty from the fall of 1911 until May 1915. "Perhaps no English institution," Ollard wrote, "provided so grand a field for the display of his gifts." Except for the obvious time Churchill served as prime minister during World War II, his tenure at the Admiralty in many ways represents his finest period and saw his most significant accomplishments, and yet it ended suddenly in the most bitter and disappointing episode in Churchill's career. Churchill embarked on five major initiatives over his four years at the Admiralty, all discussed at various points in the main chapters of this book: the creation of a Naval War Staff, the conversion of the fleet from coal to oil and the securing of adequate oil reserves to supply the new fleet, the founding of the naval air corps, the development of the tank during World War I, and the Dardanelles offensive in Turkey. The Dardanelles offensive, as discussed in Chapter 3, led directly to his ouster from the war council. Lord Kitchener—who had not always been fond of Churchill—said to him: "Well, there is one thing at any rate they cannot take from you. The Fleet was ready."

The period from May 1915 to July 1917 was probably the lowest point in his life, not excepting the "Wilderness Years" before World War II. Years later Churchill's wife Clementine told Martin Gilbert, "I thought he would die of grief." During a part of this interlude, Churchill went off to the trenches in France to command a regiment (he referred to himself during this period as "the escaped scapegoat"), where he exhibited his usual take-charge attitude. He organized a delousing effort, took a close interest in the digging and reinforcement of trenches, and was credited with raising the morale of the troops under his command "to an almost unbelievable degree," as one of his subordinates, Jock McDavid, wrote. "No detail of our daily life was too small for him to ignore. He overlooked nothing. . . . I have never known an officer [to] take such pains to inspire confidence or to gain confidence; indeed he inspired confidence in gaining it."

In July 1917, David Lloyd-George, who had replaced Herbert Asquith as prime minister under a new coalition government several months before, brought Churchill back into the government as minister of munitions, in charge of all production of war materials. "Not allowed to make plans," Churchill reflected later, "I was set to make the weapons." The Munitions Ministry, which cobbled together at the beginning of the war all the different munitions structures for the various fighting branches, was the largest productive enterprise in history at the time Churchill assumed the reins. Chapter 4 recounts his impressive accomplishments at this post.

After the war ended in November 1918, Churchill was elevated to secretary of state for war and air. The most immediate task at hand after a large war is how to demobilize the troops. Before Churchill had taken his new office the demobilization policy had called for the release from the army of skilled personnel needed to resume key jobs back in England. But in a great many cases such people had only been in the army for a short period, which led to bitter resentment on the part of long-serving soldiers who rightly feared finding employment later if all good jobs were already taken. Mutinies and insubordination were starting to occur. Churchill therefore assumed office "with conditions of critical emergency," and immediately decided that the policy must be changed. "A broad and bold handling of the problem is required," he wrote. Churchill's new policy, which he had to force on the cabinet, discharged personnel according to length of service and age, combined with an increase in pay for those remaining in the army, so as to lessen the gap between civilian and military compensation. This arrangement worked much more smoothly and equitably than its predecessor. Over the following six months, the military discharged about 10,000 men a day.

Churchill's other large initiative in this post was Britain's intervention in the civil war in the new Soviet Union, and it was not a success. Churchill was an early and vocal foe of Bolshevism, appreciating immediately that the ideological basis of Communism would generate gangster regimes. "Of all the tyrannies in history," he said, "the Bolshevik tyranny is the worst, the most destructive, the most degrading." Churchill hoped that Britain and her war allies would directly intervene to depose the Bolsheviks, but the war-weary alliance had no enthusiasm for the idea. Churchill had to settle mostly for sending military supplies to the White Russian armies, even though Prime Minister David Lloyd-George was decidedly cold to the whole idea, which led to a lack of consistent policy. The episode became known as "Mr. Churchill's private war," and contributed to his undeserved reputation in later years as a warmonger. Churchill continued throughout 1919 and 1920 to press for more aid to the White Russians, until their defeat brought the entire untidy effort to an end. Contemporaneous with this episode, the Chanak crisis with Turkey, which Churchill was also in the middle of, also nearly brought Britain to the brink of renewed war.

Churchill moved to the Colonial Office in 1921. His restructuring of the colonial administration of the Middle East included a partition of Palestine that was to make way for the eventual establishment of Israel. The other dominating issue of his Colonial Office tenure was home rule for Ireland. But this issue was just as intractable in Churchill's time as it is today. His attempts at a moderate solution to the divisions in Ireland, though typically energetic and hopeful, proved unavailing in the end, and won him the lasting dislike of many Irish.

At the end of 1922 both Churchill and the Liberal Party suffered a massive defeat at the polls, and Churchill found himself without a seat in Parliament for the first time in more than 20 years. (At about that same time, he underwent surgery for appendicitis. He awoke, he later remarked, "without an office, without a seat [in Parliament], and—without an appendix.") He would remain out of office for almost two years, during which time he worked on his memoir of World War I, *The World Crisis*. During this time he switched by gradual degrees back to the Conservative Party, which he had left in 1905 over the issue of free trade. The decision of Liberal Party leaders to throw in their lot with the Labour Party to form a coalition government disturbed Churchill, and contributed to his move back to the Conservatives.

The Conservative Party returned to power under the leadership of Stanley Baldwin in 1924, and Baldwin stunned Churchill when he offered him the post of chancellor of the exchequer. The chancellorship, which has always been regarded as the number two position in the cabinet hierarchy, had been the job his father, Lord Randolph, briefly held and resigned from in 1886. "This fulfills my ambition," Churchill said. He still had his father's robes packed away, and resolved to wear them.

Churchill served as chancellor for nearly five years—one of the longest-serving chancellors in British history. Just as in his previous ministries, Churchill set broad themes and large projects. His first budget cut income taxes for the middle class and included new social insurance programs. He successfully fought to restrain military spending. He successfully renegotiated the payment schedule for Britain's war debts to the United States. He mediated a coal strike that had briefly become a general strike that threatened to shut down the entire economy. Though his mediation was not successful in the end, both sides credited him with a tireless good-faith effort to reach a settlement. Toward the end of his chancellorship, Churchill proposed a sweeping plan for reforming the "rating" scheme of local taxation, which was similar to the property tax in the United States. Churchill used arguments that sound very much like today's "supply side" economics, arguing that lowering local tax rates would stimulate industry and employment, and generate higher revenues for the central treasury. "Debt and taxation lie like a vast wet blanket cross the whole process of creating new wealth by new enterprise," Churchill wrote. Another aspect of Churchill's plan finds its echo in our own time: he proposed to make up for the loss of local government revenue with "block grants" from the national treasury, which at the time enjoyed a surplus. This plan met with tough opposition from his fellow cabinet members (especially the minister of health—Neville Chamberlain). "Everyone but you is frightened at its boldness and magnitude," one of his exchequer staff members wrote to him. Churchill continued to press for the idea, but the Conservative government was voted out of office in 1929 before it could be implemented.

By far the most notable act of Churchill's chancellorship was Britain's return to the gold standard in 1925. The return to the gold standard led to a deflation that imposed considerable dislocation on the British economy, and is thought to have contributed to the onset of the Great Depression a few years later. John Maynard Keynes, who advised Churchill against the return to gold, later wrote a broadside titled "The Economic Consequences of Mr. Churchill." The return to gold has always widely been considered one of Churchill's greater mistakes, and it is often supposed that he rushed into the decision with haste and with little forethought. In fact, the return to the gold standard had been set to occur in legislation passed several years before Churchill became chancellor, so not going back to gold would have required a difficult act of new legislation to undo the previous law. Moreover, Churchill moved slowly and deliberately toward the decision, which was almost unanimously backed by the leading public and private financiers of the time. Despite this near-unanimity of opinion, he still expressed misgivings about returning to gold. He argued at the outset against a hasty decision, and demanded to be convinced of the merits of the idea, and went along only reluctantly, even in the face of strong opinion. He later came to regret the decision, writing in 1932 that

"I have gone the whole hog against gold. To hell with it! It has been used as a vile trap to destroy us." He also said "I hope we shall hang Montagu Norman" (the leading Treasury official who had urged the gold standard upon Churchill) and that he would turn "King's evidence" against Norman.

After Churchill and his party were defeated in the election in 1929, Churchill's life and career took a major turn. He split from his party's position over India (then seeking its first steps toward independence), and then later and more famously he split from his party, after it had returned to power once again under Baldwin in 1932, over the issue of rearmament. Throughout the 1930s, Churchill was estranged from his own party, a period known as the "Wilderness Years." His relentless criticism of England's feeble response to the growing Nazi menace in Germany was not welcomed, though it had some effect on national policy.

During his "Wilderness Years," Churchill maintained a noteworthy career as an author and investor. He became a director of two companies, R. & J.H. Lea Limited and Mann George Depots Limited, both coal transport firms. He also invested heavily in the stock market, especially in the United States, and was in New York during the October 1929 crash, during which his own stock holdings were largely wiped out. At other times, however, Churchill enjoyed more success as a stock investor.

Most remarkable about Churchill in the 1930s was his prodigious literary output. Even in the midst of the Parliamentary debates about rearmament and the growing German threat that absorbed so much of Churchill's energy and attention, he was able to write more than a million words. He produced the four-volume biography of his ancestor Marlborough, and he had written more than 500,000 words of his *History of the English-Speaking Peoples* by the outbreak of the war in 1939. (The book was finally published, also in four volumes, in 1956.) This extraordinary output amid the immense personal and political stress of the time was possible only through his skillful use of research assistants and a devoted secretarial staff. He supplemented his income from books with hundreds of newspaper columns and magazine articles, which were widely published both in England and abroad, and for which he was well-paid. His total earnings from writing between 1929 and 1939 were over £125,000—a sum in today's dollars that would be over $4 million. "A very strange way to earn a living!" he once remarked. Since he dictated most of his books and articles, he also once quipped, "I lived from mouth to hand."

Churchill finally rejoined the cabinet in September 1939, when the war with Germany broke out and his rival and party adversary Neville Chamberlain realized that Churchill had to be brought back into the government. Churchill served as First Lord of the Admiralty over the next nine months, until a political crisis that coincided with the German invasion of France compelled Chamberlain's resignation as prime minister, whereupon Churchill became prime minister for the duration of the war. Just two months after the end of the war, Churchill suffered the humiliation of being voted out of office in a landslide election. During the next six years as leader of the opposition, Churchill wrote his six-volume memoirs about World War II, for which he won the Nobel Prize for Literature. The income from his postwar writings finally provided the financial security he had always sought.

Churchill became prime minister again in 1951 and served until 1955, but by this time he was advanced in years (he was 80 when he finally resigned), and obviously was not facing the same kind of supreme trial that World War II presented. His main object during his second premiership was to broker some kind of lasting settlement of the Cold War between the West and the Soviet bloc. He proposed to hold a meeting of the major powers "at the summit" (it is from Churchill that the phrase *summit meeting* originated), but his designs were frustrated by both American and Soviet opposition. He suffered a serious stroke during his second premiership, and eventually resigned in 1955, turning over leadership to his longtime understudy Anthony Eden. In many ways, his second premiership was a long curtain call.

SOURCE NOTES

Preface

"A man's life must be nailed. . ." from MEL, p. 113; "writing a book is an adventure" from Halle, p. 233.

Introduction

Welch epigraph from *Harvard Business Review*, Sept./Oct. 1989, p. 113; "I found that the word [strategy]" from Drucker, *Innovation*, p. 209; "there were very few things in military administration" from Gilbert, *Churchill: A Life*, p. 134.

Chapter 1

"An accepted leader" epigraph from SWW, vol. 2, p. 29; "genius . . . cannot be acquired" from MHLT, vol. 2, p. 114; "the ability to foretell" from Halle, p. 40; "what is the good" from Halle, p. 260; "I decline utterly to be impartial" from MG, vol. 5, p. 174; "This is no time for windy platitudes" from MG, vol. 5, p. 1252; "some form of Gestapo" from Cannadine, p. 274; "If you wanted nothing done" from Halle, p. 44; "Occasionally he stumbled over the truth," "two nurses," "more like a rabbit," and "He is the only case" from Halle, pp. 113, 98, 118, 275; "Winston thinks with his mouth" from RSC, vol. 2, p. 329; "He is the sort of man" from MG, vol. 5, p. 173; "In the course of my life" from Halle, p. 145; "Ponder and then *act*" from MG, vol. 4, p. 67; "Whatever course was decided upon" from MG, vol. 6,

p. 129; "It is in my character" from Lewin, p. 267; "Winston was often right" from Manchester, vol. 1, p. 20; "Most great exploits" from Gilbert, *Churchill's Political Philosophy*, p. 78; "How easy to do nothing" from MG, vol. 3, p. 707; "There are plenty of good ideas" from MG, vol. 3, p. 810; "I never worry about action" from MG, vol. 6, p. 935; "The difficulty is not winning" from MG, vol. 7, p. 524; "Power, for the sake of lording" from SWW, vol. 2, p. 28; "The pursuit of power" from MHLT, vol. 2, p. 521; "had not the experience" from ATD, p. 162; "The longer you look back" from Manchester, vol. 1, p. 12; "History, for Churchill" from Kemper, p. 65; "Churchill's dominant category" from Berlin, p. 4; "How strange it is" from MG, vol. 5, p. 319; "the greatest historical work" from Jaffa, *Statesmanship*, p. ix; "the unfathomable mystery" from MHLT, vol. 2, p. 270; "preserved an imperturbable demeanor" from MHLT, vol. 2, p. 116; "The issue in this matter" from MHLT, vol. 2, p. 304; "What a strange thing" from MG, vol. 4., p. 525; "In a war involving" from MHLT, vol. 2, p. 280; "The mental process of a general" from MHLT, vol. 3, p. 94; "is bound to weaken confidence" and "None must go" from MG, vol. 6, p. 449; "studied attentively" from MHLT, vol. 3, p. 537; "We know of no similar defiance" from MHLT, vol. 2, p. 423; "Instead of seeking" from MHLT, vol. 2, p. 551; "made candor serve" from MHLT, vol. 3, p. 342; "The decision to give this blood transfusion" from SWW, vol. 2, p. 345; "This decision was one of the hardest" from ATD, p. 172; "Circumstances alone decide" from MHLT, vol. 2, p. 113; "this extraordinary quality" from MHLT, vol. 2, p. 564; "Those who are charged" from TA, p. 17; "an efficient and successful administration" from MG, vol. 7, p. 466; "Churchill scrutinizes every document" from MG, vol. 6, p. 556; "Have you done justice" from SWW, vol. 2, p. 602; "On no account reduce" from SWW, vol. 6, p. 584; "There was no detail" from MG, vol. 6, p. 1020.

Chapter 2

"Curse ruthless time" epigraph from Carter, p. 3; it "had always been his custom" from MG, vol. 5, p. 66; "I want this government" from MG, vol. 5, p. 70; "the passive matrix" from MG, vol. 6, p. 146; "the great need we have" from Comp. Vol. 5, part 1, p. 1006.

Chapter 3

"We must learn from misfortune" from MG, vol. 5, p. 995; "In all great business" from TA, p. 17; "Politics are almost as exciting" from Halle, p. 40; "the total absence" from MG, vol. 7, p. 380; "We had a long Cabinet" and "We had a Cabinet this morning" from Comp. Vol. 3, part 1, pp. 49, 78; "In Cabinet he was markedly silent" from GC, p. 140; "We ought not to drift" from MG, vol. 3, p. 226; "I think the War Council" from MG, vol. 3, p. 230; "all our calculations" from MG, vol. 3, p. 529; "The numbing hand of Asquith" from MG, vol. 3, p. 753; "Are there not other alternatives" from MG, vol. 3, p. 226; "Battles are won" from TWC, vol. 1, p. 464; "History will vindicate the conception" from MG, vol. 3, p. 564; "Nothing leads more surely" from MG, vol. 3, p. 554; "few sensations are more painful" from RW, p. 61; "My one fatal mistake" from MG, vol. 3, p. 488; "leads to weak and faltering decisions" from MG, vol. 7, p. 554; "every war decision" from MG, vol. 3, p. 554; "Whatever course was decided upon" from MG, vol. 6, p. 129; "What you have no right" from MG, vol. 7, p. 139; "five distinct truths" and "It is not right" from Comp. Vol. 3, part 2, p. 1570; "a sound and farsighted conception" from James, p. 87; "the only imaginative strategic idea" from MG, vol. 8, p. 1074.

Chapter 4

"There ought to be ways" epigraph from Gilbert, *Churchill: A Life*, p. 141; "Churchill himself was no administrator" from ATD, p. 51; "that administration was not" from James, p. 70; "Churchill's colleagues" from MG, vol. 4, p. 894; "Churchill was an administrative colossus" from Schoenfeld, p. 68; "his personal private office" from Berlin, p. 20; "The efficiency of a war Administration" from SWW, vol. 2, p. 33; "Churchill always likes to take the lead" from RSC, vol. 2, p. 431; "Winston commandeered" from RSC, vol. 2, p. 258; "I thought it better" from TA, p. 71; "I don't know how fluent he is" from MG, vol. 3, p. 107; "*someone* has to take responsibility" from MG, vol. 3, p. 434; "There is one epicycle of action" from Comp. Vol. 2, part 3, p. 1641; "It is easier to give direction" from SWW, vol. 1, p. 330; "it is simply darkening counsel" from Schoenfeld, p. 63; "The growth of the Ministry" from TWC, vol. 2, p. 1174; "It is indispensable" from Comp. Vol. 4, part 1, p. 138; "Are you sure you have a big enough machine" from Comp. Vol. 4, part 2, p. 471; "Ministerial responsibility" from MG, vol. 4, p. 505; "I am sure there are far too many committees" from SWW, vol. 2, p. 500; "Let me have a complete list" from MG, vol. 6, p. 797; "presided efficiently" from ATD, p. 159; "All had to be explained" and "I shall not be willing" from SWW, vol. 1, pp. 470, 510; "The days of mere coordination" from MG, vol. 6, p. 324; "It is my practice" from Schoenfeld, p. 50; "It was in his combined capacity" from MG, vol. 6, p. 322; "Another indispensable feature" from Comp. Vol. 4, part 2, p. 472; "I must emphasize the need" from MG, vol. 7, p. 165.

Chapter 5

"You cannot build a staff" epigraph from Comp. Vol. 2, part 3, p. 1485; "By and large" from Drucker, *Frontiers*, p. 119; "While Churchill could undervalue" from Schoenfeld, p. 55; "Perhaps it is because" from RW, p. 57; "There is a great opportunity" from WP, vol. 2, p. 268; "we cannot afford" and "such prejudices" from SWW, vol. 2, p. 534; "no mere question of seniority" from MG, vol. 7, p. 451; "advised about him" from TWC, vol. 1, p. 65; "Harsh, capricious, vindictive" from GC, p. 337; "There is no doubt" and "Favoritism is the secret" from TWC, vol. 1, p. 54; "This liquid fuel problem" from RSC, vol. 2, p. 590; "At the Admiralty Fisher served" from MG, vol. 3, p. 185; "We made the agreement" from TWC, vol. 1, p. 57; "My bringing Fisher back" from GC, p. 338; "At any rate it seems to me" from Blake & Louis, p. 386; "It is essential" from MG, vol. 4, p. 896; "He pretended" and "agony of reluctance" from ATD, pp. 53, 142; "I don't suppose" from MG, vol. 6, p. 675; "take the rough with the smooth" from MG, vol. 6, p. 1052; "Churchill never let down his staff" and "As he spoke" from ATD, pp. 241, 245; "You are not presenting me" from SWW, vol. 2, p. 501; "Do not think of making a case" from MG, vol. 6, p. 162; "He came well prepared" from MG, vol. 6, p. 157; "In any sphere of action" from SWW, vol. 2, p. 28; "even the military student" from RW, p. 165; "Proceeding by design" from MG, vol. 4, p. 72; "Step by step is a valuable precept" from RSC, vol. 2, p. 591.

Chapter 6

"If we look back" epigraph from TA, p. 15; "It is always wise" epigraph from Halle, p. 266; "It is perhaps a good thing" from MG, vol. 7, p. 20; "All these questions can be settled harmoniously" from Comp. Vol. 4, part 1, p. 383; "In a tale of war" from RW, p. 165; "The questions to be decided" from RW, p. 172; "The old wars were decided" from MG, vol. 3, p. 567; "This is a Steel War" from Comp. Vol. 4, part 1, p. 160; "All war is hazard" from Comp. Vol. 3, part 2, p. 1570; "You cannot win" from MG, vol. 3, p. 411; "What does the nation expect" from MG, vol. 3, p. 490; "We have never done anything" from MG, vol. 6, p. 189; "The offensive is three or four times" from MG, vol. 6, p. 92; "I have two or three projects" from MG, vol. 6, p. 133; "The negative in our counsels" from MG, vol. 7, p. 21; "It is far better" from MG, vol. 6, p. 181; "The effect of a 24-hour delay" from MG, vol. 6, p. 311; "Countless and inestimable" from RW, p. 143; "A true sense of proportion" from MG, vol. 6, p. 1076; "If things never turn out" from MG, vol. 3, p. 685; "Sometimes right things" from MG, vol. 7, p. 3; "You cannot be content" from MG, vol. 3, p. 434; "The entire foundation" and "It may well be" from Cannadine, p. 345; "Churchill had trained himself" from MG, vol. 6, p. 36; "Only one link in the chain" from Gilbert, *Churchill: A Life*, p. 827; "I never look beyond" from MG, vol. 3, p. 509; "It is only with some difficult" from MG, vol. 7, p. 12; "the insidious argument" from MG, vol. 6, p. 133; "The maxim 'nothing avails'" from MG, vol. 7, p. 273; "All politics are series" from RW, p. 104; "The Prime Minister" from ATD, p. 191; "never could see when" from MG, vol. 7, p. 1285; "sometimes there are great advantages" from MG, vol. 8, p. 15; "Guidance in these matters" from MG, vol. 7, p. 1140; "I allowed differences" from SWW, vol. 6, p. 535; "It is always a good thing" from MG, vol. 8, p. 637; "If we manage it well" from MG, vol. 7, p. 25.

Chapter 7

"Of all the talents" epigraph from Comp. Vol. 1, part 1, p. 816; "I did not begrudge" from SWW, vol. 2, p. 28; "Must you fall asleep" from Halle, p. 225; "Winston has spent" from Manchester, vol. 1, p. 32; "These impromptu feats" from *Savrola*, p. 108; All "Scaffolding of Rhetoric" cites from Comp. Vol. 1, part 2, pp. 816–819; "terminological inexactitude" from RSC, vol. 2, p. 163; "I hope the term" from Halle, p. 149; "accommodation unit" from Halle, p. 247; "Every offensive lost its force" from MG, vol. 4, p. 81; "like chasing a quinine pill" from Halle, p. 65; "Everything, he assured us" from Cannadine, p. 121; "I do not begrudge" from Cannadine, p. 143; "Make your minds perfectly clear" and "I sympathize with General" from Halle, pp. 152, 187; "Nothing of any consequence" from TWC, vol. 1, p. vii; "I am a strong believer" from SWW, vol. 2, p. 30; "This was a deliberate attempt" from MG, vol. 6, p. 322; "This is the sort of pedantry" from Halle, p. 140; "This paper by its very length" from Manchester, vol. 1, p. 31; "Please look at this mass of stuff" from WP, vol. 2, p. 1086; "It is sheer laziness" from ATD, p. 146; "It is our intention" from MG, vol. 8, p. 501; "Brevity" from WP, vol. 2, p. 636; "their ability to express" from Comp. Vol. 2, part 2, p. 1311; "Because of a shortage" from ATD, p. 253; "Pennywise," "Pox Brittanica," and "the socialist dream" from Halle, pp. 128, 49, 247; "This seems now to be" from ATD, p. 20; "In these dark days" from WP, vol. 2, p. 187; "The activities of the Duke" from MG, vol. 6, p. 700; "Let it be clearly understood" from SWW, vol. 2, p. 30.

Chapter 8

"Even ordinary life" epigraph from TWC, vol. 1, p. 685; "The central problem" from Schoenfeld, p. 45; "It is not always" from RSC, vol. 2, p. 335; "Mr. Asquith was" from GC, p. 150; "We owed a good deal" from Blake

& Louis, p. 135; "Since Churchill left" from MG, vol. 3, p. 581; "I am one of those" from Addison, p. 110; "Laugh a little" from MG, vol. 3, p. 651; "It is a crime to despair" from MG, vol. 5, p. 995; "Meanwhile, never flinch" from Cannadine, p. 351; "Live dangerously" from MG, vol. 5, p. 422; "When you get to" from GC, p. 89; "It is no use" from MG, vol. 6, p. 58; "I rejoice with the brilliant" from TA, p. 313; "In my belief" from Halle, p. iii; "The idea that he was rude" from MG, vol. 6, p. 1151; "The overriding impression" from Gilbert, *In Search*, p. 170; "He would at intervals" from ATD, p. 25; "I do not harbor malice" from MG, vol. 4, p. 907; "I certainly think" from MG, vol. 5, p. 1115; "This would be a foolish" from MG, vol. 6, p. 569; "It fell to Neville" from Cannadine, p. 194; "He and his colleagues" from Dangerfield, p. 261; "Oh no, I wouldn't" and "It only remains" from MG, vol. 8, pp. 108, 109; "I could not accept" from Halle, p. 214; "Every night" from ATD, p. 112; "The First Lord submits" from MG, vol. 6, p. 7; "We do not shrink" from MG, vol. 6, p. 142; "I cannot recollect" from ATD, p. 235; "I would rather be right" from ATD, p. 28; "A Statesman in contact" from TA, p. 39; "you need not expect" from Gilbert, *Churchill's Political Philosophy*, p. 86; "Human beings do not" from MG, vol. 6, p. 662; "Change is the master key" from TA, p. 297; "For every purpose" from MEL, p. 81; "My dear man" from MG, vol. 8, p. 255; "Tell the truth" from MG, vol. 5, p. 451; "It is because things have gone badly" from MG, vol. 7, p. 50.

Chapter 9

"There are plenty" epigraph from MG, vol. 3, p. 810; "We know enough" from TA, p. 274; "Once a week" from Addison, p. 128; "The agitation for" and "I like Sir Arthur" from Comp. Vol. 2, part 2, pp. 1312, 1321; "The technical training for war" and "a proper staff" from Comp. Vol. 2, part 1, pp. 1305, 1480; "To commit the navy" from TWC, vol. 1, p. 102; "Wouldn't it be simpler" from MG, vol. 3, p. 625; "After losing" from MG, vol. 3, p. 706; "Don't familiarize the enemy" from Comp. Vol. 3, part 2, p. 33; "My poor 'land battleships'" and "these suggestions" from MG, vol. 3, p. 810; "gilded wiseacres" from TWC, vol. 1, p. 525; "it was primarily due" from MG, vol. 3, p. 537; "It is only possible" from MG, vol. 5, p. 259.

Chapter 10

"A Government should" epigraph from Halle, p. 272; "It was quite the most uncomfortable lunch" from MG, vol. 3, p. 632; "This is *not* the last" from Roberts, p. 144; "Seldom can a Prime Minister" from ATD, p. 49; "I hope it is not too late" from MG, vol. 6, p. 314; "There now occurred" from MG, vol. 6, p. 419; "And then he said" from WP, vol. 2, p. 183; "There then occurred a demonstration" from SWW, vol. 2, p. 88; "It is the moral" from Blake & Louis, p. 327; "Human judgment may fail" from MG, vol. 8, p. 409; "I have always been against" from Halle, p. 213; "Civilization is the state of society" form Gilbert, *Churchill's Political Philosophy*, p. 109; "Moral force" from Halle, p. 115; "I found no comfort" from MEL, p. 276; "My conviction that" from MG, vol. 3, p. 610; "I know I am going" from MG, vol. 8, p. 514; "If I had to live," "Modern conditions," and "I do not seek to tread" from TA, pp. 2, 256, 19; "nobody left his presence" from ATD, p. 154.

Appendix

"Churchill made it his business" from RSC, vol. 2, pp. 189, 309; "I am glad to say" and "All S. African business" from Comp. Vol. 2, part 2, p. 680; "I know the Colonial Office" from RSC, vol. 2, p. 234; "No one could ever have" and "When I accepted Churchill" from RSC, vol. 2, p. 201; "Dimly across gulfs of ignorance" from Comp. Vol. 2, part 2, p. 755; "Consider the peculiar case" from RSC, vol. 2, p. 29; "Socialism wants to pull down wealth" from RSC, vol. 2, p. 255; "An extreme socialist policy" and "I distrust profoundly" from James, ed., vol. 1, pp. 875, 912; "will remove from the Court" from RSC, vol. 2, p. 278; "The establishment of Labor Exchanges" from Comp. Vol. 2, part 1, p. 853; "The Temperance Address shows" from Jaffa, *Crisis*, p. 249; "These methods of regulating" and "There ought to be" from Addison, pp. 78, 80; "Your position has now risen" from RSC, vol. 2, p. 349; "The myth of Tonypandy" from Rose, p. 95; "I consider that every workman" from Addison, p. 146; "The navy of that day" and "perhaps no institution" from Blake & Louis, p. 376; "No detail of our daily life" from Gilbert, *In Search*, p. 92; "A broad and bold handling" from MG, vol. 4, p. 185; "Of all the tyrannies in history" from MG, vol. 4, p. 278; "without an office" from Halle, p. 78; "Debt and taxation" from MG, vol. 5, p. 238; "I have gone the whole hog" from MG, vol. 5, p. 425.

Key

Comp. Vol.—Documentary companion volumes to official biography.

ATD—*Action This Day: Working with Churchill*

GC—*Great Contemporaries*

MEL—*My Early Life*

MG—official biography by Martin Gilbert

MHLT—*Marlborough: His Life and Times*

RSC—official biography by Randolph Churchill

SWW—*The Second World War*

TA—*Thoughts and Adventures*

TWC—*The World Crisis*

RW—*The River War*

WP—*Churchill War Papers*

Other items refer to authors of volumes in Bibliography.

BIBLIOGRAPHY

Addison, Paul. 1992. *Churchill on the Home Front, 1900–1955*. London: Pimlico.

Arnn, Larry P. 1986. *Churchill as Minister of Munitions: A Study of Domestic Decision-Making in War Time*. Unpublished dissertation, Claremont Graduate School, Claremont.

Berlin, Isaiah. 1981. "Winston Churchill in 1940." In *Personal Impressions*. London: Hogarth Press.

Blake, Robert, and William Roger Louis, eds. 1993. *Churchill: A Major New Assessment of His Life in Peace and War*. New York: Norton.

Cannadine, David, ed. 1989. *Blood, Toil, Tears and Sweat: The Speeches of Winston Churchill*. Boston: Houghton Mifflin.

Carter, Violet Bonham. 1965. *Winston Churchill: An Intimate Portrait*. Orlando: Harcourt, Brace.

Churchill, Randolph S. 1966. *Winston S. Churchill: Youth, 1874–1900*. Boston: Houghton Mifflin. (Vol. 1 of official biography.)

Churchill, Randolph S. 1967. *Winston S. Churchill: Young Statesman, 1901–1914*. Boston: Houghton Mifflin. (Vol. 2 of official biography, cited in notes as RSC vol. 2.)

Churchill, Randolph S., and Martin Gilbert, eds. 1969–1983. *Winston S. Churchill*. London: Heinemann. (Documentary companion volumes to the official biography. 5 vols. Cited in notes as Comp. Vol. 1, etc.)

Churchill, Winston S. 1937. *Great Contemporaries*. London: Thornton, Butterworth. (Cited in notes as GC.)

Churchill, Winston S. 1933–1938. *Marlborough: His Life and Times.* 4 vols. London: Harrup. (Cited in notes as MHLT.)

Churchill, Winston S. 1930. *My Early Life: A Roving Commission.* New York: Scribner. (Cited in notes as MEL.)

Churchill, Winston S. 1899. *The River War.* London: Eyre & Spottiswoode. (1987 Sceptre edition cited in notes as RW.)

Churchill, Winston S. 1956 (1900). *Savrola.* New York: Random House.

Churchill, Winston S. 1948–1954. *The Second World War.* 6 vols. London: Cassell. (Reprint Society edition cited in notes as SWW.)

Churchill, Winston S. 1932. *Thoughts and Adventures.* London: Thornton, Butterworth. (Cited in notes as TA.)

Churchill, Winston S. 1923–1929. *The World Crisis.* 6 vols. London: Thornton, Butterworth. (1938 Oldhams 2 vol. edition cited in notes as TWC.)

Colville, John. 1985. *The Fringes of Power: 10 Downing Street Diaries, 1939–1955.* New York: Norton.

Dangerfield, George. 1961 (1935). *The Strange Death of Liberal England, 1910–1914.* New York: Capricorn Books.

Drucker, Peter F. 1986. *The Frontiers of Management.* New York: Harper-Collins.

Drucker, Peter F. 1985. *Innovation and Entrepreneurship: Practice and Principles.* New York: HarperCollins.

Gilbert, Martin. 1991. *Churchill: A Life.* New York: Henry Holt.

Gilbert, Martin. 1981. *Churchill's Political Philosophy.* Oxford: The British Academy.

Gilbert, Martin. 1994. *In Search of Churchill: A Historian's Journey.* New York: Wiley.

Gilbert, Martin. 1971–1988. *Winston S. Churchill.* Vols. 3–8 of official biography begun by Randolph Churchill. London: Heinemann. (Cited in notes as MG vol. 3, etc.)

Gilbert, Martin, ed. 1993–1995. *The Churchill War Papers.* 2 vols. (Companion volume to official biography containing World War II documents). New York: Norton. (Cited in notes as WP.)

Halle, Kay, ed. 1985. *The Irrepressible Churchill*. London: Robson Books.

Jaffa, Harry V. 1959. *Crisis of the House Divided: An Interpretation of the Lincoln-Douglas Debates*. Chicago: University of Chicago Press.

Jaffa, Harry V., ed. 1981. *Statesmanship: Essays in Honor of Sir Winston S. Churchill*. Durham, N.C.: Carolina Academic Press.

James, Robert Rhodes. 1970. *Churchill: A Study in Failure*. Cleveland: World.

James, Robert Rhodes, ed. 1974. *Winston S. Churchill: His Complete Speeches, 1897–1963*, 6 vols. London: Chelsea House.

Kemper, R. Crosby III, ed. 1996. *Winston Churchill: Resolution, Defiance, Magnanimity, Good Will*. Columbia: University of Missouri Press.

Lamb, Richard. 1991. *Churchill as a War Leader: Right or Wrong?* London: Bloomsbury.

Lewin, Ronald. 1973. *Churchill as Warlord*. New York: Stein & Day.

Manchester, William. 1983–1988. *The Last Lion: Winston Spencer Churchill*. 2 vols. New York: Little, Brown.

Roberts, Andrew. 1994. *Eminent Churchillians*. New York: Simon & Schuster.

Rose, Norman. 1994. *Churchill: The Unruly Giant*. New York: Free Press.

Schoenfeld, Maxwell William. 1971. *The War Ministry of Winston Churchill*. Ames: Iowa State University Press.

Wallin, Jeffrey D. 1981. *By Ships Alone: Churchill and the Dardanelles*. Durham, N.C.: Carolina Academic Press.

Wheeler-Bennett, John, ed. 1968. *Action This Day: Working with Churchill*. Includes memoirs from Lord Normanbrook, Sir John Colville, Sir John Martin, Sir Ian Jacob, Lord Bridges, and Sir Leslie Rowan. London: Macmillan. (Cited in notes as ATD.)

ACKNOWLEDGMENTS

I FIRST VISITED Churchill's birthplace, Blenheim Palace, when I was 13 years old, so in the first instance I should thank my parents, to whom I owe unlimited gratitude for so much else in life, for the initial inspiration to study Churchill. This book really evolved over a period of several years, the result of innumerable conversations with a wide range of people on the subject of what Churchill has to teach us today. In alphabetical order, they include: Larry P. Arnn, president of the Claremont Institute for the Study of Statesmanship and Political Philosophy, for the use of parts of his extensive collection of Churchill literature, as well as for years of casual remarks about Churchill, many of which found their way into this account; Kelly Clark, a public man now passing through his own "wilderness years," for the many long conversations about the possibilities of exercising Churchillian virtue today; David DesRosiers, probably the only man in the world bearing a tattoo of Churchill, for a number of pithy observations that appear in these pages; David Green, for his always acute observations and suggestions on the subject; Harry V. Jaffa, Henry Salvatori Emeritus Professor of Political Philosophy at Claremont McKenna College, and president of the Winston S. Churchill Association, one of my principal teachers in graduate school, for illustrating brilliantly the essential connection between classical political teaching and Churchill's modern practice of it; and California State Assemblyman Tom McClintock, a public man whose own "wilderness years" are now over for good, for exemplifying Churchillian resolve and pluckishness.

Others who deserve mention for their practical involvement in this project include: Steven Martin, my enthusiastic editor at Prima Publishing, and Kevin Heverin and Tracy Claggett of ICS Press, who applied the practical pressure on me to turn a mere idea into a serious plan of action, and who then offered a number of sensible midcourse corrections along the way; Sally Pipes, president of the Pacific Research Institute for Public Policy (my current outpost), for her indulgence as I worked on this project, no doubt to the detriment of pressing matters at the office; and of course my wife Allison, who cheerfully indulged the usual impositions of reading over and correcting countless drafts of each chapter.

INDEX